MISSION-MINDED SKITS

David C. Cook
transforming lives together

D1418537

getting the best out of teen drama

MISSION-MINDED SKITS
Published by David C. Cook
4050 Lee Vance View
Colorado Springs, CO 80918 U.S.A.

David C. Cook Distribution Canada
55 Woodslee Avenue, Paris, Ontario, Canada N3L 3E5

David C. Cook U.K., Kingsway Communications
Eastbourne, East Sussex BN23 6NT, England

Written by Cynthia Miller
Cover Design: Kevin Mullins
Interior Design: Helen Harrison/Ya-Ye Design
Illustrations: BMB Design

Scripture quotations, unless otherwise noted, are taken from the HOLY BIBLE, NEW INTERNATIONAL
VERSION® . Copyright © 1973, 1978, 1984 by International Bible Society. Used by permission of Zon-
dervan. All rights reserved. Scripture quotations marked KJV are taken from the King James Version of
the Bible (Public Domain). Scripture quotations marked MSG are taken from The Message. Copyright ©
1993, 1994, 1995, 1996, 2000, 2001, 2002. Used by permission of NavPress Publishing Group.

ISBN 978-0-7814-4559-7

First Printing 2008
Printed in the United States

1 2 3 4 5 6 7 8 9 10

CONTENTS

INTRODUCTION

Short-term mission trips are a leading avenue to catapult today's youth into an authentic, adventure-filled experience of sharing the gospel of Christ with the world! Drama is an exciting way youth can participate—no matter what their level of previous training or gifting. Short mimes and skits—creatively presented—add a dimension of time, place, and emotion to grab audience attention and draw the nonbeliever to the gospel. Mission skits and mimes should always be followed up with either conversations or a message to nonbelievers where the gospel is presented.

These skits have been used in many types of overseas settings: in the African bush for school children, as street ministry, at church services in Asia, for a European youth class, at coffeehouses, at youth retreats, and as sermon illustrations. Likewise, they have been used and adapted for various stage settings: in a field with no mikes, on a crowded sidewalk with a hand-held mike, with and without an interpreter, on both a very small and large stage, and with large or small teams.

You will have the ability to adapt these skits to many situations. Suggestions are provided for use or adaptations for the cultural environment as well as tips for stage setup, props, and cast expansion. As you read through these scripts, pray for open hearts of the people who will see and hear the message of Christ presented by your drama team. Get ready for an adventure!

"Let your light so shine before men, that they may see your good works and glorify your Father in heaven" (Matt. 5:16).

PREPARE FOR SPONTANEITY

A Word about Props, Cast, and "Making Do"

Though cloudy, the air was hot and sticky that day on the island of Okinawa. A steady stream of rain began to fall as the team walked from door to door, leaflets in hand. The carefully worded flyers gave news of a concert being held at the church where Japanese neighbors could come and experience American music, food, and fellowship. The missions team hoped and prayed that neighboring Japanese people would be eager to practice their English speaking skills with the American "gaijin" (foreigners). As the team prepared to perform dance, worship songs, and a skit called "Living Water" (p 109), we realized there was no room on stage for our team. So we would have to perform the skit on the floor at the front of the crowded room. Although the skit was difficult to see from the back, our weeks of practice proved faithful, and it was pulled off without a hitch. The night resulted in twelve decisions for Christ . . . a relatively large number considering that in the spiritually closed country of Japan, Christians only make up one percent of the population.

When your team prepares to travel out of the country, partner with an indigenous church or mission organization and pack for less than ideal conditions. Things don't always go as planned. Bags containing props get lost, buses break down, schedules might—and often do—change. Flexibility in the midst of these inconveniences is key. Impress this on your team. What director doesn't want the perfect cast, perfect sound system, perfect props, and perfect setting? Unfortunately we live in a fallen world where mikes don't work, actors get sick, and your 7'x7' "stage" is poorly lit. What to do? The show must go on! An African bowl, a Mexican sombrero, or a Russian shawl can add authenticity to your story. Keep your cool and make do with what you have. Remind your team why they are there and to "walk in love." Make Romans 12:12 your motto: "Be joyful in hope, patient in affliction, faithful in prayer." Remember 2 Corinthians 5:20: your trip is more about who you are in Christ than what you do! You are Christ's ambassadors.

You will find an overview page for each skit that includes the Time, Props, Target Audience, Difficulty Level, Synopsis, Cast, Topic, and Customization ideas. When performing drama in a foreign country, consideration should always be given to language interpretations and cultural customs.

The Target Audience will help you choose skits that will be most effective for the people you are ministering to. Japan, for instance, does not have a translated word for sin. Sin, to the Japanese, refers to crime . . . so it is challenging to convey the message of Jesus' forgiveness of sins. People in war-torn areas of the world do not struggle with the same issues as Americans, such as materialism, overeating, burnout, and time-management. Third-world countries more typically contend with famine, violence, rejection, the orphaned and widowed, the practice of witch-craft, and animism. Surprisingly, however, many people in European countries also practice occultism. For instance, in France, the fifty thousand full-time practitioners of the occult outnumber the thirty-five thousand known Christian missionaries. There is an area in northern Italy where Satanism is ac-tive, and the region is often referred to as the graveyard of missionaries.

Communicate with your indigenous church contact and research the Internet for things people in that culture would find offensive (women wearing pants, certain hand gestures, women dancing, crossing your legs, etc.) and make adjustments to the skit so cultural blunders won't distract the audience from being receptive. Find out what religions are practiced in the area so you can tailor your witnessing. Here is a list of the most predominant religions in the world.

Five Major World Religions
Biblical Christianity
Buddhism
Hinduism
Islam
Judaism

Others
Primitive religions (animism, witchcraft, voodoo, etc.)
Baha'ism
Jainism/Sikhism
Taoism/Confucianism
New Ageism

How to Customize
The great thing about being flexible when entering another culture is the opportunity you have to utilize your creativity! God is the creator of the universe and has given some of that creativity to us! Most of these skits are fully customizable and will have

suggestions for changes like adding or taking away cast members, interjecting foreign language, changing a scene, or adding props. Your skits can also be adapted for performances here at home for your youth group or church, children's church, street evangelism, or more.

Rehearsals

There are a number of ways to hold rehearsals before a mission trip. Here are a few suggestions for scheduling. Six weeks prior to the mission trip, schedule rehearsals two times per week. Hold a one- to two-hour session each time, depending on the number of skits. We suggest having four to six skits practiced and ready to perform for most two-week mission trips. One or two of your skits might never be performed at all, so make your team aware of this possibility and stress flexibility (See "Prepare for Spontaneity" section.). Another option is to schedule ten total practices: five days a week for two weeks. Always leave the week prior to departure open to allow time for packing and spending with family. Parent/teen relationships should always be supported and encouraged by youth leaders.

Speaking

At times you may find your skit has to be performed without mikes. Teach your actors to prepare as if there were no mikes, to speak clearly, loudly, and with good

intonation (See "Terms to Know."). A flat, monotone voice that can't be heard from more than a few feet away will not deliver the message and will cause the audience to lose interest quickly. Voices can carry farther if actors learn to speak from the diaphragm instead of from the throat.

Mime

There are a number of narrated mimes in this book. Encourage the cast to use exaggerated body language, facial expression, and movement around the stage to keep the audience interested. Feel free to add music to the background of mimes. Pay attention to hand positioning. Have actors practice with various props, and then remove them to make the movements more accurate and convincing. For instance, if the actor is holding a glass, have him practice with the glass and then try removing it.

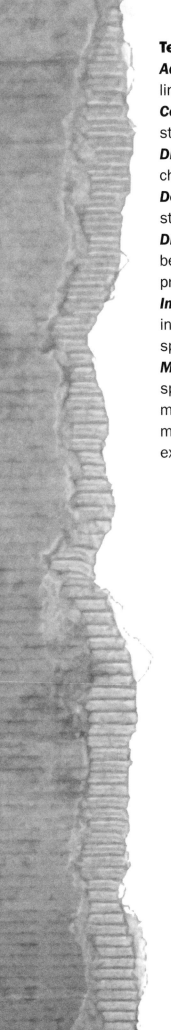

Terms to Know

Ad-lib—when an actor improvises his lines

Center stage—the very center of the stage

Dialogue—conversation between characters, spoken from the script

Downstage—the very front of the stage

Dress rehearsal—practice as it will be performed before an audience, props included

Intonation (Inflection)—the variation in tone that rises and falls when speaking

Mime—a performance with no spoken words. Character and message are conveyed with body movement, gestures, and facial expressions

Monotone—unvarying, dull quality of voice when speaking, with no rise and fall of tone

Rehearsal—practice of scenes prior to performance

Soliloquy—actor speaks lines as if to himself

Script—text of the skit to be acted out

Stage left—the actors' left as they stand onstage, facing the audience

Stage right—the actors' right as they stand onstage, facing the audience

Upstage—the very back of the stage

Do You Know?

Synopsis: "Do You Know" is a strong statement about many of the prophecies that came true concerning the birth, death, and resurrection of Jesus. The speaking quality of your actors should not be monotone, as this will leave your audience unmoved. Actors must use voice inflection and hand gestures, speaking "popcorn" style for this to have the desired effect.

Target Audience: Adults and youth. Particularly for people who practice Islam or Judaism, since they have such a keen awareness of Jesus

Topics: Salvation, Prophecies of Jesus

Cast: Four good actors who have good intonation and strong voices

Props: None

Time: 3 minutes

Difficulty Level: Moderate

Customize: This is a powerful skit, especially if your actors can project over the sounds of the audience/crowd. If their voices are simply not loud enough, use microphones.

Do You Know?

Opening Scene: *(Four people enter stage left and all stand downstage from stage left to stage right, equally spaced apart, facing audience. Arms should be at sides. Leave room in front to take three steps forward.)*

Person 1: Do you know of this man?

Person 4: This radical?

Person 2: Perhaps you have heard of him, born long ago in Bethlehem.

Person 3: He grew up and performed many miracles.

Person 4: Healed the sick!

Person 2: Gave sight to the blind! *(While speaking puts hands up to eyes, takes away)*

Person 1: Brought the dead back to life! *(While speaking, moves hand from low to high)*

Person 3: He taught many things about his Father.

Person 2: He told us to . . .

Person 4: Love God. *(Holds out arms)*

Person 1: Love each other. *(Gestures toward person on right)*

Person 3: Love our enemies.

Person 2: Forgive.

Person 4: Maybe you have heard.

Person 2: His name is

Person 3: Jesus

Person 2: Jesus

Person 4: Jesus

Person 1: Jesus!

Person 3: But did you know?

Person 1: That there were over 60 prophecies?

Person 3: And over 300 references?

Person 2: About the coming of Jesus?

Person 4: Written hundreds of years before he was born?

Person 1: Before he was born.

Person 4: *(Takes a step forward while speaking)* It was prophesied that Jesus would come from Bethlehem.

Others: Jesus was born in Bethlehem. (*Person 4* *takes one step back while this line is being said.*)

Person 1: *(Takes a step forward while speaking)* It was prophesied that Jesus would be a descendent of Abraham, from the tribe of Judah and the house of David.

Others: Jesus was born a descendent of Abraham, from the tribe of Judah, from the house of David. (*Person 1* *takes one step back while this line is being said.*)

Person 2: *(Takes a step forward while speaking)* It was prophesied that Jesus would perform miracles, preach the good news.

Others: Jesus performed miracles and preached the good news. (*Person 2* *takes one step back while this line is being said.*)

Person 3: *(Takes a step forward while speaking)* It was prophesied that Jesus would be betrayed by a friend for 30 pieces of silver.

Others: Jesus was betrayed by Judas for 30 pieces of silver. (*Person 3* *takes one step back while this line is being said.*)

Person 2: *(Takes a step forward while speaking)* It was prophesied that Jesus would be accused without cause and would be silent before his accusers.

Others: Jesus was accused without cause and was silent before his accusers.
(*Person 2* *takes one step back while this line is being said.*)

Person 1: *(Takes a step forward while speaking)* It was prophesied that Jesus' hands (Looks toward left, holds out one arm as if on the cross), feet, and side would be pierced. *(During this, looks right, holds out other arm)*

Others: Jesus was nailed to a cross and hung to die. His side was pierced. (*Person 1* *hangs head down while this is being said, then puts arms down and takes a step back while* *Person 4* *says the next line.*)

Person 4: *(Takes a step forward while speaking)* It was prophesied that Jesus would be a king,

Person 3: *(Takes a step forward while speaking)* a priest,

Person 1: *(Takes a step forward while speaking)* a prophet,

Person 2: *(Takes a step forward while speaking)* the Son of God.

All: Jesus was and is a king, a priest, a prophet, and the Son of God.

Person 3: We all, like sheep, have gone astray, each of us has turned to his own way; and the Lord has laid on Jesus the sin of us all.

Person 1: *(Takes a step forward while speaking)* Have you heard?

Person 2: *(Takes a step forward while speaking)* Do you know?

Person 4: *(Takes a step forward while speaking)* Jesus, the Christ

Person 3: *(Takes a step forward while speaking)* who died for you?

End

Seekers

Synopsis: "Seekers" is about city people who feel loneliness or emptiness in the midst of daily life. This skit should flow with activity, then stop suddenly with a vignette on one actor, followed by activity and stopping again suddenly, and so on. The overall feeling should be that of a busy city. Props are minimal.

Target Audience: Adults, urban cultures in more affluent countries

Topics: Salvation, Emptiness

Cast:
Missionary: Choose your best actor—someone engaging, sincere, and convincing.
Realtor: Female working in office. Standing stage right front, notebook and pen in hand, cell phone on ear
Co-workers: One person filing papers, One person talking on the phone, others standing behind her in a group, talking loudly about their business dealings
Commuters: Three to six people walking on street far stage left
Solicitor: Man on "street" handing out flyers downstage

Props: Two cell phones, pens, paper, clipboard, flyers, Bible

Time: 4 minutes

Difficulty Level: Moderate (some difficulty getting the timing right for the street scene and transitions between "freeze" scenes and movement)

Customize:

1. You can add more people to the street scene as extras: someone selling food and people buying, someone jogging by, an artist painting, a homeless man begging. Women and men can switch characters if needed.

2. The entire scene can take place in a school. Realtor becomes student council president. Co-workers become student council members talking about weekend plans. The street scene becomes a school hall. The Solicitor will become a Janitor who
is mopping the floor and says nothing to students, but still addresses audience (he is not handing out flyers). Dialogue remains the same for all characters. Change of props: mop or broom instead of flyers.

Seekers

Opening Scene: *(Office scene, stage right. Everyone else is onstage and frozen in place. All the Co-workers are busy working and talking loudly.)*

Realtor: *(Loudly into phone)* Yes, all right, I understand. I'll send you the papers tomorrow. Thanks for the information. Good-bye. *(She hangs up, and the **Co-workers** freeze. **Realtor** looks at audience.)* Tonight I will go home, sit around, and watch some TV. I do the same thing every night. I am so lonely! *(With feeling, she looks down, then starts to write.)*

*(**Co-workers** start talking again. Someone says, "Time to go home." **Co-workers** and **Realtor** start to move through "office door" toward center stage. Have someone open "door" and let others walk through. They move to stage left and begin talking.)*

Street Scene: *(This scene needs to happen fluidly. Now there is activity all over the stage. **Commuters** enter stage right. **Solicitor** enters from stage left and moves toward center. As he stands in center, **Commuters** and **Co-workers** walk past him.)*

Solicitor: *(Attemps to hand flyers to **Commuters** and **Co-workers** as they pass by.)* Please take one. Please take one. *(Everyone on stage freezes. **Solicitor** looks at audience.)* Every day I stand here for many hours. This gets so boring. At least I have my family to go home to. My wife is a good wife. Our children work hard and do well in their studies. Even so, why do I feel so lonely? Why do I feel empty inside? It all seems so meaningless. *(Talks slowly, pausing a little between comments. People start to walk and talk again. **Solicitor** hands someone a flyer.)*

Missionary: *(Enters from stage left carrying his Bible and directs his comment to two people who are standing on the street.)* Can I talk with you about our God? *(They look at each other and nod in agreement.)* Do you believe in God?

(Everyone freezes.)

Missionary: *(Turns and takes two steps toward audience. Speaks with feeling.)* I used to be so lonely on the inside. Sure, I had lots of friends and kept busy, but, you know . . . on the inside . . . I was empty. I tried to fill my life with excitement, and I had fun, but it never lasted. I had to keep going from one thing to the next, trying more and more exciting things. I tried to find fulfillment in relationships. But after a while, no matter how great a person they were, no matter how beautiful, I ended up feeling empty again. I went from job to job, thinking money would help me. I was able to live a better life, but after awhile, I still had that gnawing emptiness that wouldn't go away.

Then . . . I met someone who said they had God living inside them, filling the emptiness! It sounded so strange, yet I knew all those years this was what I was looking for. I wanted to hear more, so he read God's words from his book and told me many amazing things . . . how God loves me, and how this same God who created everything in the world, knew about me before I was born. That he had a plan for my life that was good and meaningful and that he would take away the loneliness and forgive my sins. All I had to do was believe in him.

(Excitedly) Now I want to share this good news with everyone I meet! *(Turns toward people)* God promises that when you seek him, you will find him. He also promises he will never leave you nor forsake you. *(Turns right and left, then, loudly)* Is anyone here lonely? *(Half of the people on the street stop and look at him.)* Does anyone here feel empty? *(The other half of the people on the street stop and look at him.* **Missionary** *opens Bible, then looks around)* "I am the way, the truth and the life." God's Son, Jesus, also says, "I come that they might have life and have it to the full."

(Everyone freezes.)

End

Soccer

Synopsis: "Soccer" is a satire about two soccer teams trying to play a game where one player doesn't think the rules are absolute. Note: most countries call this sport "Football."

Target Audience: Adults, teens. For countries where there is a predominance of Relativism (the belief that there is no absolute truth – this philosophy is prevalent mostly in advanced cultures).

Topics: Sin, Absolute Truth

Cast:

Ref: The youngest kid on the team, chosen as Ref because he's not very good at soccer. He doesn't really know what he's doing. Choose youngest and shortest for this part.

Blue Striker: Good actor with good improvisation ability. Is not a team player and is insistent on his own way. He should be able to make the goal each time.

Blue Defender: Always kicks the ball to someone at beginning of play. He lets Striker lead the team.

Blue Team Extras: Stand in various positions on the field

Red Striker: Good actor with good improvisation ability. Nice guy playing his position. He is dumbfounded by the Blue Striker's attitude, a little impatient with him.

Red Midfielder: Team player, wants to have fun

Red Keeper: Team player, wants to have fun

Red Defender: Just wants to play! Kicks ball around in between plays, throws hands in the air, gestures impatiently

Red Team Extras: Stand in various positions on the field

Props: Soccer ball, two goal nets, whistle, red card (approximate size of an index card, red on both sides), Optional: shin guards and uniforms (same colored T-shirts, etc.)

Time: 10 minutes

Difficulty Level: Moderate

Customize:

If you are performing this in America, change the game to baseball. The batter (Blue Striker) swings and misses but argues with the pitcher (Red Striker), assuring him that it wasn't a strike. The umpire (Ref) is similarly ineffective. Batter says it was "a near miss, a slip-up, a good try, a challenging effort, a practice swing. Who cares anyway? I'm not hurting anyone!" You can make up similar "rule-less" scenarios for the baseball game.

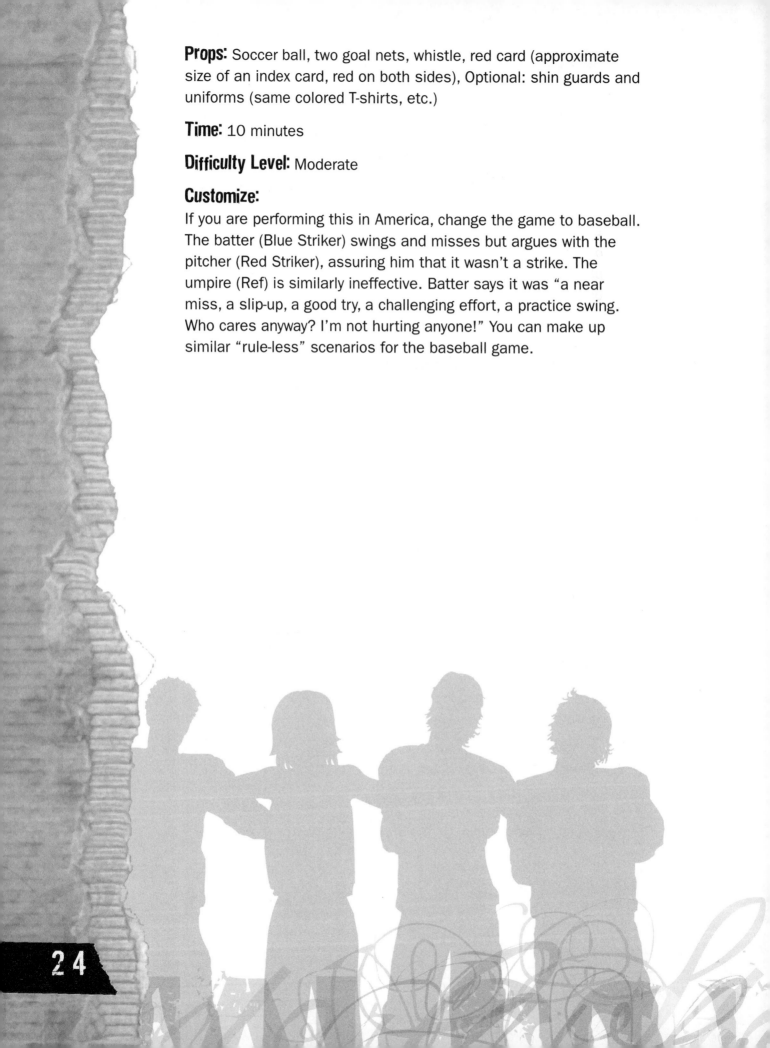

Soccer

Opening Scene: *(Seven to eleven youth playing soccer (or football). Use entire stage. Two teams huddle together separately to plan the play. Nets are at stage right and stage left.)*

*(The **Ref** stands downstage center with ball in hand. The **Blue** and **Red Striker** stand on either side of the ball. Sets ball down, steps back, blows whistle. The **Blue Striker** kicks it to **Blue Defender** behind him and then runs toward his own goal. The **Red Striker** and **Midfielder** press forward toward the blue players. The **Blue Defender** passes it back to the **Blue Striker**, who kicks it past the **Blue Goalkeeper**, into his own goal. The **Ref** blows whistle and announces a point for the Blue Team.)*

Red Striker: *(Turns to **Ref**)* Hey! What do you mean? He didn't score! That was his net! *(**Ref** looks at **Red Striker** and shrugs his shoulders.)**(To **Blue Striker**)* What are you doing? That wasn't your point!

Blue Striker: *(Holding the ball)* It's our goal and our point . . . right guys? *(Turns and looks at his teammates, who adopt various attitudes of agreement or confusion)*

Red Striker: This is where you're supposed to kick your ball! *(Points at the red goal)* You score there!

Blue Striker: Well, this time I wanted to score in our own net for a change.

Red Striker: You can't just change the rules like that! We're starting over!

Blue Striker: Fine! *(Throws ball to **Ref** and turns to his team)* Blue Team, huddle up!

*(After the huddle, all players get back into starting positions. The **Ref** puts ball down, backs away, and whistles to start play. The blue players kick it around, until it gets back to the **Blue Striker**, who picks it up and throws it to the **Blue Goalkeeper**. The **Blue Goalkeeper** throws it into his own team's goal. The **Ref** blows whistle and announces a point for the **Blue Team**. The blue players immediately start jumping up and high-fiving each other.)*

Red Team: *(Starts talking all at once)* You can't do that! What? This is ridiculous! I can't believe this!

Red Striker: *(Throws up hands in disgust)* I must be seeing things! Ref . . . what's wrong with you?

Ref:	Fine! You be the Ref then! *(Throws down his whistle and stomps off stage right)*
Red Striker:	Maybe I will! *(Picks up the whistle, blows it, and holds up red card toward **Blue Striker**)*
Blue Striker:	No way! That isn't a foul!
Red Striker:	It was the worst foul I've ever seen! What would you call it?
Blue Striker:	I call it innovative . . . helping our team . . . playing smart . . . You're making too much out of this. It's just a small change in the direction of the game.
Red Defender:	*(Yells)* Come on! Are we playing or not?
Red Striker:	OK, let's try this one more time. No "small" changes please *(Glares at the **Blue Striker**. Puts the ball down and blows his whistle)*

*(The **Blue Striker** picks up the ball and throws it to the **Blue Midfielder**, who runs toward **Red's** goal. After a few steps, he throws it back to the **Blue Striker**. He catches the ball, knocks down a red player in his way, and throws the ball into the net.)*

Red Striker:	*(Walks over to them, picks up the fallen red player, and addresses the **Blue Striker**.)* Let me guess . . . you were playing smart?
Blue Striker:	*(Smiles, shrugs shoulders)* We took you by surprise with that move, didn't we? I'm just trying to have a nice game of soccer.
Red Striker:	A nice game? I think we could have a nice game if you played the right way.
Blue Striker:	*(Takes a step toward the Red Striker)* It's all relative. Just let us play the game the way we want to.
Red Striker:	OK, let's say we let you do whatever you want . . . score in the wrong net, throw the ball with your hands, knock over your opponents. What if we play that way, too? What if we really knocked you guys around?
Blue Striker:	Well, you could if you wanted, but I don't think that would be fair.
Red Striker:	Fair? No, it wouldn't be. That's why we have rules. And you can't just change them!

Blue Striker: That may be the way you play.

Red Striker: There is no soccer without the rules. *(The rest of the Blue Team walks toward the two Strikers.)*

Red Defender: OK, that's it! We need to either play this game or quit!

(Everyone freezes.)

Red Striker: *(Walks downstage center facing audience. Speaks in a calmer tone than before.)* I think it's obvious that this game isn't going anywhere. Have you ever heard of the Striker running with the ball across the field? He refuses to admit he's wrong. Funny thing is, I've heard people react in a similar way when they don't follow the rules in their own life . . . "It's just a weakness . . . it was one slip-up . . . I do a lot of good things . . . it was a just a little white lie . . . I didn't steal it . . . I just borrowed it for a while . . . I just looked at her test for a minute . . . it really wasn't anything." The reasons go on and on. *(Pause)* I understand though, I used to do that myself.

The thing is, a sin is a sin. You see, the natural human part of us wants to make excuses. But as I found out, Christ died so we wouldn't have to make excuses. When we live by his rules and admit when we have sinned . . . he's there, ready to forgive.

End

The Prodigal (a mime)

Synopsis: The prodigal son story taken from Luke 15:11-32

Target Audience: All ages. Particularly for cultures practicing Hinduism and Buddhism. There is a similar story in Buddhist writings, but the meaning is far different. Buddhists (represented by the son in the story) believe that because they are unwise, they must suffer and endlessly wander in this world as they are reincarnated over and over again hoping to gain enough wisdom to deserve Nirvana (represented by the father in the story), which is the absence of all things, including self. This story also speaks to those cultures practicing the Hindu caste system, where the lowest regarded people are considered polluted outcasts and assigned the lowest paying jobs.

Topics: Forgiveness, Love

Cast:

Rich Father: Good acting ability, comes across as sincere and loving. Dressed in modern-day "rich" attire. Find out what clothes a wealthy man would wear in the country you are traveling to and get something similar, though fake. Nice suit, gold watch, necklace and rings. It wouldn't be wise to take expensive items into a foreign country where they can be stolen or ruined. Check out your local second-hand shops.

Youngest Son: Good acting ability, good facial expressions. Set of everyday clothes and set of ripped and dirty clothing. Take old pants and rip holes in the knees or rip half of a pant leg off. Rub T-shirt and pants in dirt.

Oldest Son: Good acting ability. Must be able to act angry, disappointed, jealous. Neat and clean, everyday clothing, clean shoes

Servants: A couple of people in very simple clothes

Harlot: Woman dressed in a long skirt wearing a scarf

Bartender: Man in everyday clothes with sleeves rolled up

Customers: Men and women of varying ages

Props: This skit can also be performed without any props or costumes (optional prop ideas listed in Customize section).

Time: 10 minutes

Difficulty Level: Moderate (acting must be exceptional)

Customize:

1. Add a number of props: reading glasses, backpack, wallet, fake money (some cultures will question throwing real money around), bucket, robe or cloak, plastic drinking glasses, long scarf, notebook, broom, cleaning cloths, bowls, table, food, trays, sandals.
2. Add inoffensive cultural dance music at the end. Servants, father, and youngest son are dancing to the music when oldest son walks in. Music stops and father talks with son, etc.
3. Add narration at the end or at different points in the story. Have the translator practice narrating the story in case there are translation questions.

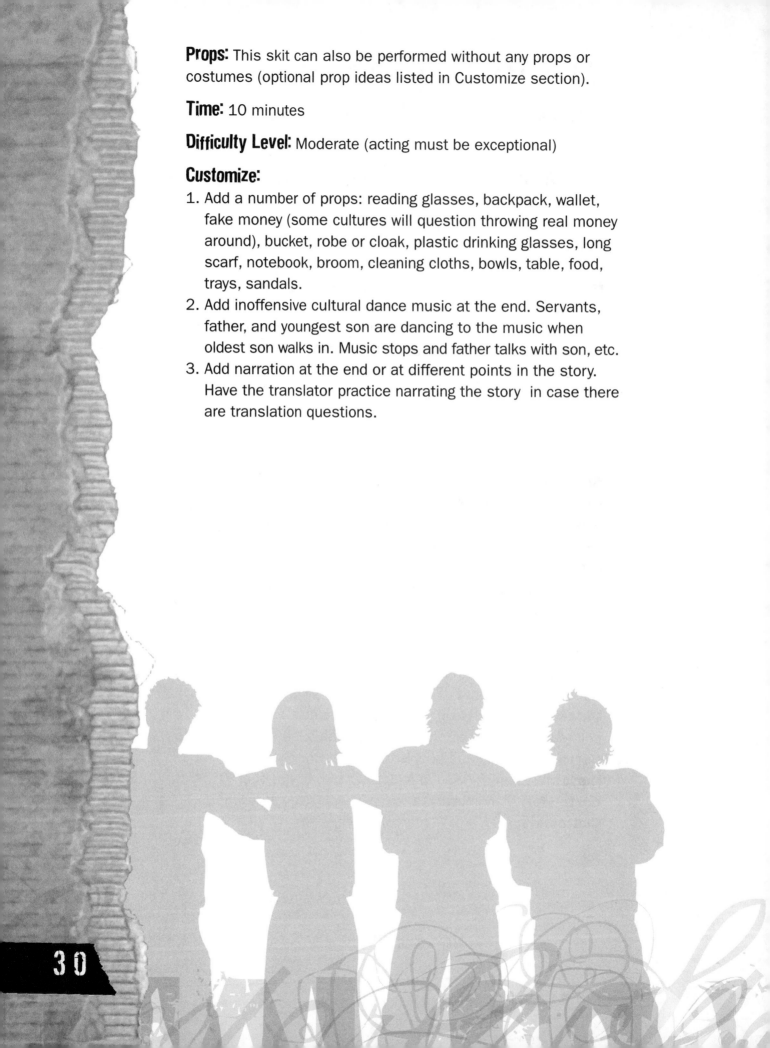

The Prodigal (a mime)

Opening Scene: (Three people are downstage center: the **Father** and two **Servants** are standing in his house. The **Father** directs the two **Servants** to sweep and clean up.)

Youngest Son: (Enters stage right and walks up to **Father**, the **Oldest Son** following and holding an accounting notebook. **Youngest Son** points at the book, showing the **Father** his portion of the inheritance.)

Father: (Puts on his glasses to see better while holding onto the book and nods head.)

Youngest Son: (Steps away and grabs backpack. Walks back over to **Father** as he motions stage left with his other hand.)

Father: (Shakes head no, points to the book they are reading while motioning him to come over and take a look.)

Youngest Son: (Stands and shakes his head no, puts his backpack on his back, and holds out his hand for money.)

Father: (Opens box and gives **Youngest Son** a handful of money.)

Youngest Son: (Stuffs money in his pocket and forcefully walks off stage left.)

Father: (Looks distressed. Takes a few steps toward stage left after his son leaves. Takes off his glasses and looks down for a moment cleaning them and thinking. Then he walks off stage right looking sad, and his **Oldest Son** follows him, shaking his head in disgust.)

Bartender & Customers: (Enter stage left. **Bartender** starts to wipe off tables, picks up a cup, holds it up to the light, and cleans it with a cloth. **Customers** mime drinking and eating.)

Youngest Son: (Enters stage left, walking tall and straight.)

Bartender: (Walks up to him and offers cup.)

Youngest Son: (Takes cup while **Bartender** fills it. **Youngest Son** drinks it in one swig and **Bartender** pours another while **Youngest Son** takes money out of his bag and pours it into **Bartender's** hand. All appear very happy and smiling.)

Harlot: (Enters stage left swinging a scarf, motions to him, walks up to him smiling. Note: Don't overdo this scene by acting or dressing suggestively. Don't touch each other, as this might be offensive to some cultures.)

Youngest Son: (Pulls out a long gold necklace and gives it to **Harlot**.)

Harlot: (Appears very happy, admires her expensive gift.)

Youngest Son: (A little drunk now, takes more money from his bag and holds hand up high, dropping lots of coins into **Harlot's** hands. They seem to laugh, as he pours money on her head. They start to wobble off stage left together. He stops and turns toward the **Customers** and laughs, throws money into the air.)

Customers: (Run over to the ground and pick up money.)

Youngest Son and Harlot: (Exit stage left together.)

Father: (Enters stage right followed by **Oldest Son**, who is holding the accounting book. **Servants** come onstage and do obvious work. **Oldest Son** watches while **Father** walks downstage center. **Father** holds hand up to his forehead and looks back and forth stage left for **Youngest Son**. **Father** clasps hands behind back, looks down. He turns and walks over to **Oldest Son** to look at the books again. **Oldest Son** talks for a few seconds, then they both exit stage right followed by **Servants**. **Father** looks back once.)

Youngest Son: (Looking dirty and poor. Now wearing rags. Barefoot and has dirt on his face. Hair is messy. Walks on slowly from stage left, stooping over and carrying a heavy bucket. He throws the contents to the pigs and sets the bucket down. Puts his hands in his pockets and pulls them inside out . . . empty. He flops down where he is. He grabs his stomach, picks up the bucket, and pours a few drops into his mouth. He takes out a photo he has in his back pocket. He stares at it and starts to cry. Wipes face with his arm, and then crawls offstage left.)

Father: (Similar to earlier scene with **Father** looking for **Youngest Son**, except **Oldest Son** is not with him. **Servants** are doing work. **Father** walks to far side of stage right looking at his books.)

Youngest Son: (Slowly crawls on from stage left.)

Father:	*(Turns, sees **Youngest Son**, and takes a step forward.)*
Youngest Son:	*(Stops and looks up at **Father**. **Father** runs over to **Youngest Son** excitedly and lifts him up. **Father** hugs **Youngest Son** once, looks at him, and hugs him again.)*
Youngest Son:	*(Gets back down on knees and holds clasped hands up to **Father**, shaking them. **Father** interrupts and smiles, pulls **Youngest Son** up, and puts his arm around his shoulder. They walk to **Servants** while **Youngest Son** cries and wipes his eyes.)*
Servants:	*(All come running.)*
Father:	*(Gesticulates as if ordering **Servants** to prepare a banquet. They run every which way all over the stage, grabbing bowls and plates. They set the table and run on and offstage with food, carrying trays, etc.)*
Oldest Son:	*(Enters stage right and stops. Puts hands on hips and points finger at **Youngest Son**, looking angry. Makes animated gestures, pointing at **Father**, the accounting book, etc.)*
Father:	*(Smiling, walks over to **Oldest Son** and points to his outfit head to foot to indicate that **Oldest Son** is rich and blessed. Then he points to **Youngest Son** to show the difference in appearance between the two. Walks over to **Youngest Son** and gives him a big hug. **Servant** brings **Father** a robe, and he wraps **Youngest Son** in it. **Servant** puts sandals on his feet. **Father** then motions for both sons to eat at the banquet table.)*

(Everyone freezes.)

End

Hearing God (a narrated mime)

Synopsis: A man named Jonathan is looking for God. After observing his neighbors looking for God in nature, Jonathan meets Jesus.

Target Audience: Children, people who practice Shintoism and animism which endorse worshiping and/or make offerings to different gods and spirits of the natural world

Topics: Seeking God, Salvation

Cast:
Narrator: Choose someone who is a great storyteller and who can speak loudly and with good inflection. Should stand stage left or offstage
Wild Person: Character behaves oddly and runs out into the rain. Choose someone who uses exaggerated body language and is comfortable onstage.
Bowing Person: Choose someone who has funny facial expressions and is good at physical comedy.
Jonathan: This person will climb on his neighbor's back. Should have good facial expressions and an ability to speak loudly
Jesus: Will have a few lines. Good acting ability required
Blind Woman: Healed by Jesus
Neighbor: Needs to be able to carry Jonathan on his shoulders
Crowd: Several followers and townspeople

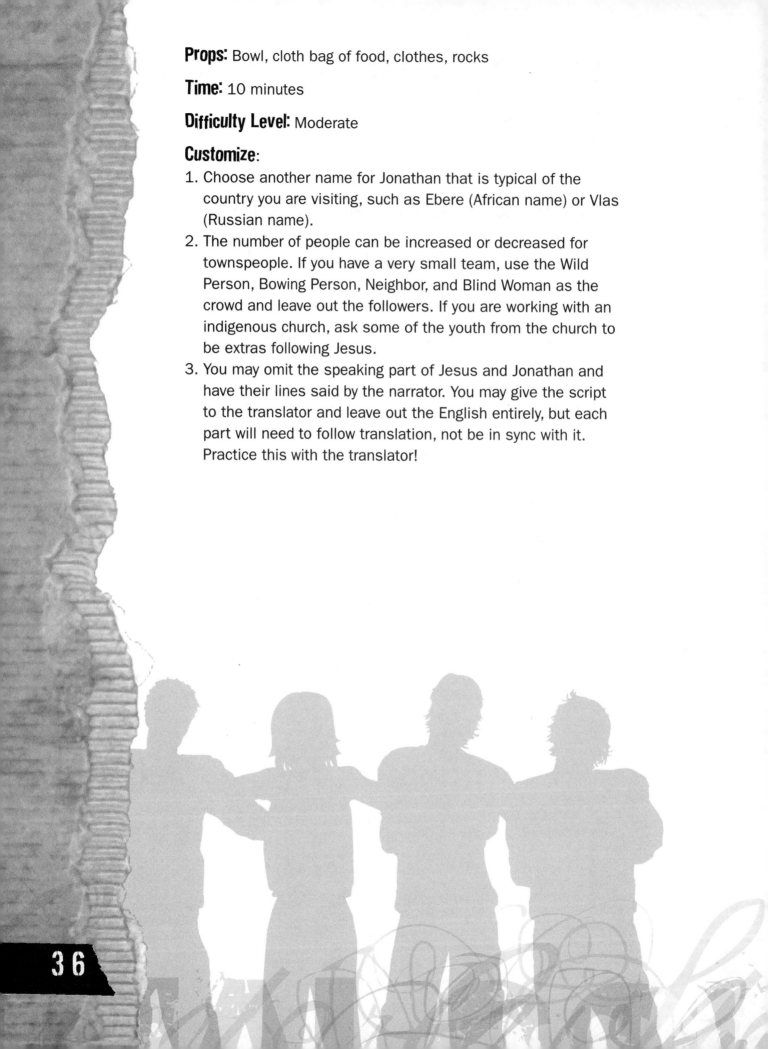

Props: Bowl, cloth bag of food, clothes, rocks

Time: 10 minutes

Difficulty Level: Moderate

Customize:

1. Choose another name for Jonathan that is typical of the country you are visiting, such as Ebere (African name) or Vlas (Russian name).

2. The number of people can be increased or decreased for townspeople. If you have a very small team, use the Wild Person, Bowing Person, Neighbor, and Blind Woman as the crowd and leave out the followers. If you are working with an indigenous church, ask some of the youth from the church to be extras following Jesus.

3. You may omit the speaking part of Jesus and Jonathan and have their lines said by the narrator. You may give the script to the translator and leave out the English entirely, but each part will need to follow translation, not be in sync with it. Practice this with the translator!

Hearing God (a narrated mime)

Opening Scene: (*Wild Person, Bowing Person,* and *Jonathan* are standing stage right, a few feet from each other, facing the audience, heads down, frozen.)

Narrator: There were once three people who wanted to hear from God. The first person thought that the all-powerful God would only speak through the wind during a thunderstorm. So she decided the only way she could get God's attention was to go out into a storm, shout, and wave her hands wildly in the air and jump up and down so that God would notice her and speak to her.

Wild Person: (*Looks up at sky, holds hand out to see if it's raining, and then takes a few steps "outside." She then starts to wave hands in the air wildly as though waving to God in the sky to get his attention, shouts (no words), and jumps up and down.*)

Narrator: She soon got very tired and wet, but she wanted to hear from God more than anything else, so every day she ran outside and sat waiting for a storm to come along.

Wild Person: (*Wipes her arms of water, wrings her clothes in exaggeration, goes back inside and sits down to think. After a few seconds, she gets up, scans the skies for rain and then starts jumping again. Repeat this over and over. Stays stage right. Continues until it's time for her exit.*)

(**Narrator** pauses briefly for action.)

Narrator: The second person thought God was part of all the trees and rocks and rivers and animals, so he decided to bow down low and worship every time he came up to a tree, a rock, a river, or an animal, believing that one of these things would speak to him as God.

Bowing Person: (*Walks up to a rock and bows down low. Stands up, takes a few steps, then sees another rock and repeats. Stays stage right. Walks and bows in a circle. Continues until it's time for his exit.*)

Narrator: He soon got very tired of stopping to bow down and realized that he would not accomplish much during the day if he continued to bow down every time he saw a rock, a tree, a river, or an animal . . .but he continued to do this because he was convinced that God would speak to him.

(**Narrator** pauses briefly during action.)

Narrator: The third person was also seeking God, and wondered how to talk with him. His name was Jonathan.

Jonathan: *(Stands with head in hand, thinking)*

Narrator: Now, Jonathan was a wise man in his village. So, as he walked past the two people and observed what they were doing he said, "If God is watching, I wonder what he thinks of this. Surely God is not the storm. Surely God is not inside a rock!" He knew in his heart that something had created the bees, the land, and the animals and people; he was sad not to find God here.

*(In sync with the **Narrator, Jonathan** walks over to the **Wild Person** and **Bowing Person** and shakes his head at each. **Wild Person** and **Bowing Person** exit stage left.)*

Narrator: So Jonathan went home and wondered how he could ever find and talk with God.

Jonathan: *(Walks through a "door" and sits down, stays stage right.)*

Narrator: One day a foreigner came into Jonathan's village. The foreigner spoke in the town center and drew a crowd.

Jesus: *(Enters stage left, followed by a **Crowd**, including the **Blind Woman**. **Jesus** stands upstage and talks with everyone standing near him. A total of six people encircle **Jesus**, who is still visible to the audience. **Jesus** is "talking" (silently) and motioning with hands.)*

Narrator: Rumors were told of how the man had healed the sick in other villages, so a Blind Woman was brought to the foreigner.

*(At the word "rumors," two of the people in the crowd start to walk the **Blind Woman** up to **Jesus.**)*

Narrator: He said, "Today your faith has made you see." (**Jesus** mouths this in sync with **Narrator**.) As he touched her eyes, they were healed.

*(**Jesus** acts this out. **Blind Woman** gets excited and runs around to different people, smiling and gesturing towards **Jesus**.)*

Narrator: A Neighbor ran to Jonathan and told him that the foreigner claimed to be God's very own Son, and that he performed a miracle!

Neighbor: *(Runs to **Jonathan**, talking excitedly. They run back together.)*

Narrator: Jonathan could not get through the crowd of people to meet God's Son. But he wanted to hear him speak! So he asked his Neighbor to lift him on his shoulders.

*(Now everyone listening to **Jesus** encircles him. **Jonathan** runs back and forth but can't get through the people, so he gets on **Neighbor's** shoulders.)*

Narrator: When he saw the man, he thought, "This doesn't look like God's Son."

*(**Jonathan** looks at the audience, motioning with his hands in sync with **Narrator**.)*

Narrator: But the foreigner looked up at him and said, "Jonathan, come down from there. I must eat at your house today." Jonathan jumped down as he thought, "How does he know my name?" So he went to him and said, "Look, Lord! Right here and now I believe you are God's Son! Please tell me what God has to say to me!"

*(**Jonathan** jumps down and pushes his way through the crowd to **Jesus**. The audience must be able to see **Jesus** in front. He then gets down on one knee. **Jesus** and **Jonathan** mouth the words being said.)*

Narrator: And Jesus said to him . . .

Jesus: *(Says this out loud) Today salvation has come to you. For I came to seek and to save what was lost. (As he speaks, **Jesus** puts hand on **Jonathan's** shoulder.)*

Jonathan: *(Says this out loud) Lord, what must I do now? (Gestures questioningly with hands)*

Jesus: *(Says this out loud) Turn from your sins and let me give you a clean heart. Come and follow me and you will learn everything about my Father's will for your life. (**Jesus** slowly turns to exit stage left, and all except **Jonathan** and **Neighbor** follow him.)*

Narrator: So Jonathan ran home and gave all his possessions to his Neighbor and ran back to follow Jesus. He spent the rest of his days talking with God and doing everything that God told him.

*(**Jonathan** happily runs home, followed by his **Neighbor**, grabs a bowl, bag of food and clothes, hands them to his **Neighbor** and runs after **Jesus**, who is now walking away with the crowd. **Neighbor** quickly looks at the stuff in his arms, looks at the crowd leaving, looks at the audience, drops everything and runs after them.)*

End

Who Do You Listen To?

Synopsis: A sobering revelation of how our thoughts and actions can be influenced by Satan if we allow him to, and the consequences of doing so.

Target Audience: Teens. Speaks to people who practice primitive religions (i.e., animism, witchcraft, and voodoo) because of their belief in evil spirits. Particularly applicable to those in third-world countries where education is a means to rise above poverty, but where there are many personal battles to overcome in order to finish their education.

Topics: Spiritual Warfare, God's Peace

Cast:
Demon: Dressed all in black
James: Youth not wanting to attend school. Choose someone with good acting ability.
Sarah: Youth also struggling to attend school. Choose someone with good acting ability.

Props: Black clothes, gloves, shoes, black and red face paint for Demon, mirror, Bible, purse, backpack

Time: 5 minutes

Difficulty Level: Easy. However, do practice this with the spotlight effect.

Customization Ideas:

1. This can be performed without a spotlight.
2. Choose names native to the country you are visiting.
3. This can be easier to perform with two demons, one each for James and Sarah.

Who Do You Listen To?

Opening Scene: (*Sarah* is standing stage left, *James* is standing stage right, and *Demon* is standing upstage center, slightly behind them. All have heads down, frozen. Lights out, if possible. Spotlight will alternate between *James* and *Sarah*. *Demon* moves between them, slightly crouched the whole time, taking one or two steps forward and then back, coming out of the shadows.)

(*Spotlight on Sarah*)

Demon: (*Steps forward toward Sarah, slightly behind and speaking close to her head.*) Don't go to school today.

Sarah: I really don't want to go to school today.

(*Light out. Spotlight on James*)

Demon: (*Steps right, toward James, slightly behind*) Don't go to school today.

James: Maybe I won't go to school today.

(*Light out. Spotlight on Sarah*)

Demon: (*Moves to Sarah*) Just skip this once.

Sarah: I could miss just this once. Maybe Ann will skip classes with me.

(*Light out. Spotlight on James*)

Demon: (*Moves to James*) Missing one day won't matter.

James: It's OK to miss one day. My grades aren't that great, but one day won't matter.

(*Light out. Spotlight on Sarah*)

Demon: (*Moves to Sarah*) You don't do well in school.

Sarah: I'm not going to get good grades anyway. (*Snapping out of it*) Wait—why am I saying that? I really think I need to go. I need to keep working on my subjects so I can graduate. I have a dream of someday becoming a nurse.

(*Light out. Spotlight on James*)

Demon: (*Moves to James*) No one likes you anyway.

James: No one talks to me anyway. No one likes me. I don't fit in.

*(Light out. Spotlight on **Sarah**)*

Demon: *(Moves to **Sarah**)* You will never become a nurse. You won't succeed in life.

Sarah: I'm not sure if I'll graduate with good grades . . . No, I really believe God will help me! He's done so much for me already. Let's see, what's that verse?

*(Light out. Spotlight on **James**)*

Demon: *(Moves to **James**)* You are ugly, and people don't like you.

James: *(Turns to look at mirror)* Look at my face! I'm ugly! I can't go looking like this!

*(Light out. Spotlight on **Sarah**)*

Demon: *(Moves to **Sarah**)* You don't need to look that up.

Sarah: Where is my Bible? Here it is!

*(Light out. Spotlight on **James**)*

Demon: *(Moves to **James**)* You can lie and say you feel sick.

James: I can tell them my stomach hurts too much. I need to stay home . . .

Demon: You can tell them it will be too hard.

James: I'll say that it will be too hard to go. Then I'll sneak out with Sam instead.

*(Light out. Spotlight on **Sarah**)*

Demon: *(Screams)* No-o-o-o-o, don't pick up the Bible! *(Backs away)*

Sarah: Here it is, Psalm 34:4 "I sought the lord, and he answered me; he delivered me from all my fears." Where is that other verse . . . *(Finds passage)* I think it's in Philippians . . . chapter 4 . . . verse 13. "I can do all things through Christ, who strengthens me." *(Looks away from book)* I can do all things with your help, Lord. *(Bows head to pray)*

Demon: *(Screams)* No-o-o-o, don't pray-y-y-y! *(Backs further away)*

Sarah: Lord, please give me courage to finish school. Help me to study hard and be disciplined. Lord you have helped me all of my life . . . forgive me for the times when I haven't trusted in you.

*(Lights fade out during prayer. She keeps head bowed. Spotlight on **James**)*

Demon: *(Moves to **James**)* Maybe you can be sick the rest of the week.

James: I know! I'll skip for the next few days! I'll say I'm just too sick . . . that I'm too sick to work on my studies! I'll go tell them now. *(Makes his clothes look rumpled and stoops over, holding stomach and looking sick)*

Demon: *(Looks menacing and hunched over as he follows **James** off stage right)*

*(Spotlight on **Sarah**)*

Sarah: *(Still praying)* In Jesus' name, Amen. *(Quietly hums a worship song while she grabs her backpack, puts her Bible in it, and walks off stage left.)*

End

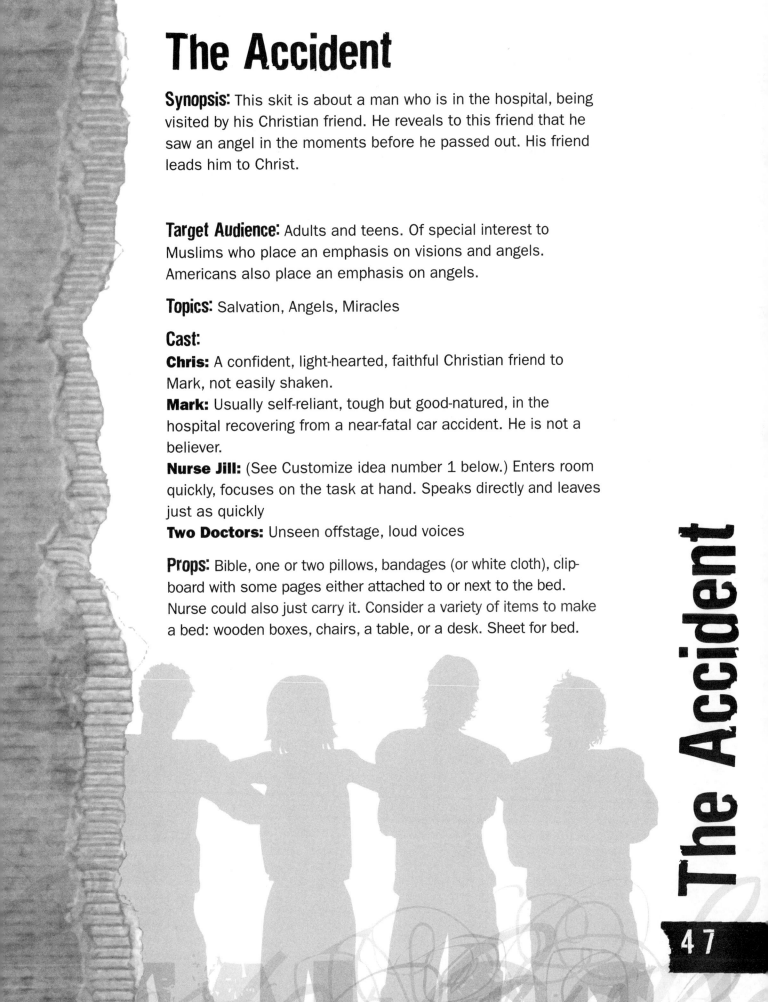

The Accident

Synopsis: This skit is about a man who is in the hospital, being visited by his Christian friend. He reveals to this friend that he saw an angel in the moments before he passed out. His friend leads him to Christ.

Target Audience: Adults and teens. Of special interest to Muslims who place an emphasis on visions and angels. Americans also place an emphasis on angels.

Topics: Salvation, Angels, Miracles

Cast:
Chris: A confident, light-hearted, faithful Christian friend to Mark, not easily shaken.
Mark: Usually self-reliant, tough but good-natured, in the hospital recovering from a near-fatal car accident. He is not a believer.
Nurse Jill: (See Customize idea number 1 below.) Enters room quickly, focuses on the task at hand. Speaks directly and leaves just as quickly
Two Doctors: Unseen offstage, loud voices

Props: Bible, one or two pillows, bandages (or white cloth), clipboard with some pages either attached to or next to the bed. Nurse could also just carry it. Consider a variety of items to make a bed: wooden boxes, chairs, a table, or a desk. Sheet for bed.

Time: 5 minutes

Difficulty Level: Easy with two good actors.

Customize:

1. If you are ministering in a specific Muslim country, find out if women hold the position of nurses. If not, make this a male nurse. Including obvious cultural offenses in skits in order to make a point will introduce too many distractions to hearing the gospel.

2. Add a nurse or two who walk in with Nurse Jill. They should straighten bed sheets and re-arrange pillows, then walk out with her. Completely bandage up one leg and one arm.

3. Change setting. This scene can take place where the accident occurred. The Nurse can instead be a Paramedic. A spinning, flashing "police" light would be great in the background as well as a medical box (toolbox will work), and Mark's head is bandaged. Have two guys hold a stretcher with Mark lying on it.

The Accident

Opening Scene: *(Two **Doctors** talk in "hall" unseen by audience. **Mark** is resting in bed with eyes shut. Make sure the audience can see the scene. Lay **Mark** on a table or two chairs, center stage.)*

Doctor 1: `Is he going to make it?`

Doctor 2: Yes, he has fractures and breaks all over his body, with severe trauma to the head, but he's conscious now.

Doctor 1: He's lucky to be alive!

*(**Chris** walks in and sits or stands next to **Mark**.)*

Chris: *(Leans over and touches **Mark** on the shoulder)* Hey, Mark . . . you awake?

Mark: *(Opens eyes)* Hey Chris . . . what's up?

Chris: You've been out for a long time, bro. How 'ya feelin'?

Mark: Actually, my head is pounding.

Chris: *(Smiling)* Yeah, you look like a mummy wrapped in all those bandages, man.

Mark: *(Sarcastically)* Thanks for the encouragement!

Chris: Man, how'd you end up like this? Someone said you left work late.

Mark: I took another shift, so I worked late that night. I was so tired, then . . . I couldn't believe it . . . it happened so fast. This guy came out of nowhere, driving right towards me! They say it was a pickup truck.

Chris: What'd you do?

Mark: I turned the wheel as hard as I could, went into a spin, and all I remember thinking was . . . this is it! My life is over. Then I remember saying out loud, "God help me" . . . *(Pause)* Why would I say that? I don't believe in God.

Chris: Do you remember when I was talking to you about God and I told you God gives every person a conscience because he wants to have a relationship with everyone he's made?

Mark: Yeah . . . maybe. *(Looks down)* But that's not all . . . I haven't told anyone this . . .

Nurse Jill: *(Walks in stage left)* S-o-o-o, how are you feeling? *(Holds a clipboard and writes some notes as she talks)*

Mark: I have one massive headache, but other than that . . . great!

Nurse Jill: *(Looks at her watch as she checks his pulse)* Your pulse is good. *(Talks as she walks offstage left)* I'll be back in a few minutes.

Mark: *(Leans over to make sure she's gone. Grabs **Chris'** arm and tries to sit up.)* OK . . . right after I called out to God I saw this bright light and . . . don't laugh . . . I swear to you . . . I saw wings!

Chris: Whoa, careful there. *(Makes him lie back down)* You saw wings? *(Laughs)* Like—butterfly wings or what?

Mark: I know—it sounds crazy.

Chris: *(Jokingly)* I think you've been hit on the head pretty hard.

Mark: I'm telling you, I really saw wings!

Chris: What happened next?

Mark: Well . . . I could see this . . . angel shielding me. And, in that instant, I felt . . . calm. It was really weird, but I knew I was going to be OK. Next thing I knew, I was on the ground, and the paramedic was asking me if I could say my name, and then I guess I just blacked out. I can't believe I lived through this! I am one lucky man!

Chris: *(Seriously, shaking his head)* It's not luck; it's a miracle.

Mark: A miracle? . . . So here's the question: Did God send an angel to protect me? If he did, why?

Chris: I think he did, Mark. In the Bible, Psalm 91:11 says God commands his angels to watch over us.

Mark: But I don't understand why God would send an angel to protect me. An angel didn't even save Jesus when he was hanging on the cross. He was God's prophet, yet God didn't save him.

Chris: Yeah, but remember I told you Jesus died willingly for our sins. Jesus didn't want God to save him! It was all part of God's plan to save us. Jesus took the pain and suffering of our sins upon himself so we could have a right relationship with God.

Mark: But I don't know if I can accept that my sins would be forgiven, completely, forever.

Chris: Remember the peace you felt before you were hit? You can have that peace all the time if you only believe in Jesus.

Mark: Like you?

Chris: Yeah, man, like me. It's amazing.

Mark: Remember when we saw *The Passion*? *(Note: The Passion was widely seen in the Mideast.)* I couldn't understand how anyone could take that kind of pain. *(Pause)* If he really did that willingly, he must really love . . . *(Trails off)*

Chris: You, Mark. (Pause) Do you think you're ready to say that prayer now . . . accepting him as your Savior?

Mark: *(Looks down at his hands, then up at **Chris** and smiles)* I'm ready.

*(**Chris** and **Mark** bow their heads. Lights out.)*

End

Jonah: Part 1—On the Run

Synopsis: Humorous adaptation of Jonah and the Fish

Target Audience: Christian teens (see Customize idea number 1 on the next page)

Topics: Disobedience, Prejudice

Cast:
Jonah: Use your best male actor for this part.
Narrator: Anyone who can speak loudly and well
Captain: Can be a male or female
Crew Members: Any number to swab the deck and prepare for launch. Crew can have ropes tied through beltloops on pants, be barefooted, wear bandanas on heads, and roll up pants midcalf.

Props: Jonah's clothing, backpack, paper tickets, coins, several beach balls. Optional: ropes, bandanas

Time: 10 minutes

Difficulty Level: Medium (Everyone must sway back and forth in sync to convey being on a ship in a storm and keep this up until Jonah is tossed overboard.)

Customize:

1. Christian youth living in non-Christian parts of the world need extra encouragement to continue in the faith and become strong Christian leaders for their communities. Plan to lead a two-day youth retreat with the church or organization you are working with. While this takes much upfront organization, drama, dance (depending on culture), games, worship, testimonies, and messages can be a powerful way to ignite the passion of youth from both countries! This skit works well for that setting.

2. This can be a large or small cast. You can combine the lines of the crew to adapt for a smaller cast size.

3. If performing this outdoors and in non-drought countries, an extra or two can throw water onto the deck (both stage right and stage left) every few minutes during the storm. He can also throw a bucket of water onto Jonah as he's being tossed in the ocean.

Jonah: Part 1—On the Run

Opening Scene: (*Jonah is alone onstage, pacing back and forth downstage center.*)

Narrator: This is the story of Jonah. God spoke to Jonah and told him to speak to the people who lived in the great city of Nineveh and warn them of the outcome their sinfulness would have. Jonah didn't want to go . . .

Jonah: (*Yelling*) What am I going to do? God himself, Lord of the Universe just asked me, Jonah, to go down to Nineveh and warn them! They'll think I'm nuts! They won't listen! What a waste of my time! I've got to get out of here! (*Pause*) I know, I'll pack up and go to Tarshish. (Rushes around and throwing a few shirts into a bag) Maybe God will forget about me. Nineveh! Those people are awful! I do not relate to them at all! (*Grabs his now-full bag and walks hurriedly off stage left. Keeps walking to back of room and comes up to stage right.*)

(*Rest of cast is standing just offstage right*)

Captain: (*Steps onstage, yells*) Tickets! Tickets! Tickets to Tarshish! All a-boar-rd! Ship to Tarshish leaving in one minute!

Jonah: (*Runs up to **Captain**.*) I'll take a ticket. (*They exchange money/ticket, then **Jonah** walks downstage and mimes holding onto ship railing.*)

Entire Crew: (*Follows **Captain** onstage and starts doing variety of activity to get ship going . . . pulls ropes, picks up and moves boxes, swabs the deck, winds up rope.*)

Captain: (*Yells*) Cast off!

Jonah: (*Looking at audience*) Whew, I'm safe now. I will spend days in Tarshish on the beach. (*Suddenly starts to sway back and forth*) Wow, kind of rough out here. Think I'll take a nap. (*Walks over to stage right and lies down, going to sleep.*)

Captain: Cast off! Hey, you two!

Crew Persons: (*Walk quickly to **Captain***) Yes sir?

Captain: Hoist the sails! Fasten the jib! We're in for a big one! (*Looking at sky.*)

(Suddenly, everyone "jerks" to stage left. This is to indicate that the waves are getting rough due to the storm. Everyone starts swaying to stage right stumbling around as they walk stage left, then right, still trying to do their work. Someone gets sick over the side.)

Captain: Everyone, batten down the hatches!

Crew Person 1: *(Yell)* Let's throw cargo overboard to lighten the load!

Crew Person 2: *(Yell)* OK, I'll grab the boxes over here!

Crew Person 3: *(Yell)* I'll grab Simon! (Simon is **Crew Person 2**.)

Crew Person 2: *(Yell)* Throw yourself overboard!

Crew Person 4: *(Yell)* How about this stuff over here?!

Crew Person 5: I feel sick. *(Runs and throws up over side of ship)*

Captain: *(Yell)* Throw everything overboard! We need to lighten this load.

Crew Person 5: *(Straightens up and raises finger)* I just did! *(Throws up again over side)*

Captain: Let's cast lots to see whose fault this is!

Crew: Yeah! *(Crew grabs beach balls and throws them together in a circle. They do a funny, complicated ritual that results in balls flying everywhere. Just leave them where they fall and for the rest of the skit, kick them aside when they're in the way.)*

Crew Person 3: Hey! It's that Jonah guy! Where is he?

Crew Person 4: *(Walks over to where **Jonah** is sleeping)* Here he is! *(**Crew** runs over to him, wakes him up. Grabs him and pulls him down stage.)*

Captain: We cast lots, and you are the cause of this storm!

*(All **Crew** say these next lines at the same time.)*

Crew Person 2: Who are you?

Crew Person 4: What do you do?

Crew Person 5: Where'd you come from?

Crew Person 3: What people are you from?

Jonah: I am Hebrew, and I worship the Lord, the God of the heavens, who made the sea and the land. This is all my fault. He asked me to go to Nineveh and speak for him, but I didn't want to, so I ran away. I'm going to Tarshish!

Captain: *(Terrified, grabs **Jonah's** arm)* What have you done?

*(**Crewmates** turn to each other and start talking excitedly. Everyone talks at the same time.)*

Crew Person 1: We're doomed.

Crew Person 3: We're going to die.

Crew Person 2: This is horrible.

Crew Person 5: I feel sick *(Runs and throws up again over side.)*

Captain: *(Raises arms)* What should we do?

Jonah: Throw me overboard. The sea will calm down when I am off this ship.

Captain: *(Looks to audience)* Great idea!

Crew: *(Grabs **Jonah** and get ready to throw him overboard. If **Crew** is strong enough, have them hoist **Jonah** up in the air.)*

Jonah: Wait, you must have thought I said throw me overboard. Noooo, I said row me overboard! You know, give me a row-boat?

Captain: OK, men, you know what to do! *(Walk him over to downstage center front and throw him offstage.)* Oh great God who made the land and sea, please don't hold the death of this innocent man against us!

Jonah: *(As he's falling)* No, w-a-i-t! A rowboat! *(When on the floor in front of the stage, acts like he's drowning.)*

Crew Person 3: The sea! It's calming down!

Crew: *(Makes sounds of relief. All get down on knees to thank God.)*

Crew Person 5: *(Jumps up and yells)* Look! Jonah is being swallowed by a great fish!

(All Crew jump up and run to the edge. They point out to sea excitedly.)

Jonah: H-e-l-p!

(All Exit.)

INTERMISSION (Interject a testimony or a short message in between these two parts.)

Jonah: Part 2—SUSHI

Synopsis: Humorous adaptation of Jonah and the Fish

Target Audience: Adults, youth, and children

Topics: Witnessing, Obedience, Forgiveness

Cast:
Jonah: Use your best male actor for this part.
Messenger: Short part anyone can do
Two Prop People: Two actors to grow like vines, wave fans, and hold flashlights
Citizens: Any number

Props: Beach towel; sunglasses; sandals; long, rolled up paper to serve as a scroll; chair or table

Time: 10 minutes

Difficulty Level: Easy. The speaking parts should flow from one to another quickly.

Customize: If performing this outdoors and in non-drought countries, throw water onto the stage after the sandals are thrown. If water is unavailable, throw a bucket of small cut-up paper.

Jonah: Part 2—SUSHI

Opening Scene: *(Empty stage area)*

Narrator: The story of Jonah continues. Jonah has spent many hours in the belly of a large fish. After he's had the chance for prayer and reflection, Jonah is spit out onto the beach by the giant fish.

Jonah: *(Throws himself on the stage, his sandals follow, one at a time. Gets up, wipes himself off)* Yuck! Whale slime! *(Stamps feet, runs fingers through his hair) This is disgusting!*

Narrator: God tells Jonah to go to the great city of Nineveh and proclaim the message God gives him.

Jonah: I'm still not sure why I'm doing this, and I really didn't like being turned into sushi.

Narrator: So Jonah makes the trek to Nineveh.

Jonah: *(Grabs his sandals, puts them on, and starts walking across stage. A large group of **Citizens** who have been standing stage left are talking loudly together when he walks up. He stands on a chair or table and acts like he's speaking to them.)* Citizens of Nineveh! The Lord has given me a word for you. He says: "Forty more days, and Nineveh will be destroyed."

Citizens: *(After a long moment of silence, everyone at once wails loudly, crying, some fall to their knees covering their faces. Many pull out hankies and blow noses. **Jonah** gets down, walks a few steps away to the right. He looks at them with his hands on hips, shaking his head.)*

Jonah: What did they expect?

Messenger: *(Enters stage left, stands on the same chair and unrolls a scroll. Acts out reading the message.)*

Narrator: The king sends a messenger to read his decree. "None of you or your animals may eat or drink anything. Each of you must wear sackcloth. You must pray to the Lord God with all your heart and stop being sinful and cruel. Maybe God will change his mind and have mercy on us so we won't be destroyed."

Citizens:	*(Everyone is kneeling down quietly crying or wringing their hands.)*
Narrator:	Jonah doesn't understand why God is having compassion on them! They are so sinful! Look at the way they dress! The way they talk! They are very violent, steal from each other, get kicked out of school, go to parties and get drunk . . . they should be destroyed! *(As **Narrator** speaks, **Jonah** stands watching in disbelief. Stamps his feet, paces back and forth getting angry.)* Jonah is annoyed with God and says "I knew from the very beginning that you wouldn't destroy Nineveh! You always show love, and you don't like to punish anyone, not even foreigners." *(**Jonah** points his finger at God toward at the sky.)* Now let me die! I'd be better off dead. *(**Jonah** throws up his hands, stomps across to stage right, pulls out his beach blanket, shakes it, and lays it down. Opens umbrella and puts on his sunglasses. He sits down under it and watches the people in the city.)*
Jonah:	I'll just wait awhile. Maybe God will change his mind.
Narrator:	So Jonah waits. And it grows very hot. God causes a vine to grow for shade. But then the vine dies. *(**Prop People** enter and lie down next to **Jonah**, hold their arms up and grow as vines, then fall down dead.)* Then a strong wind comes. *(**Prop People** wave fans in front of **Jonah**.)* Then the sun beats down on him. *(**Prop People** point flashlights in his face.)*
Jonah:	*(Takes off his sandals, pulls at his neckline, and takes offf his sunglasses)* Argh! It's so hot! I want to die!
Narrator:	God then says to Jonah "Do you have any right to be angry about the vine?"
Jonah:	*(Disgustingly jumps up, holding umbrella, looking skyward, and stomps his foot)* It's so hot, and it gave me nice shade. The poor plant died in one day! I am angry enough to die myself!
Narrator:	Then God says, "Jonah, you feel sorry about the plant, though you did nothing to put it there. And a plant is only, at best, short lived."
Jonah:	I know, but . . .
Narrator:	"But Nineveh has more than one hundred twenty thousand people living in spiritual darkness. Shouldn't I feel sorry for such a great city?"

*(As **Narrator** speaks God's words, **Jonah** glares at the audience, and stalks off stage right.)*

(**Crew Persons 1 and 2** from "Jonah: Part One" walk on stage with beach balls, towels, wearing sandals, sunglasses, shirts, and shorts ready for the beach)

Crew Person 1: Ah, this looks like a nice place to get a tan. (They lay out their beach towels.)

Crew Person 2: Yeah, that trip across the sea wore me out.

Crew Person 1: What do you think ever happened to that Jonah guy?

Crew Person 2: Oh, him? Well didn't you hear? The fish spit him out, and he went to Nineveh like God told him to.

Crew Person 1: You don't say!

Crew Person 2: Yeah, I also heard he still didn't have a very good attitude.

Crew Person 1: You don't say! After all he went through . . . and we went through, you think he'd get the message. (Starts laughing)

Crew Person 2: (Laughs along) Did you see the look on his face when that fish came up and swallowed him? (Both have a fit of laughter, holding stomachs.)

Crew Person 1: (Laughing . . .) A row boat! (Uses arms to act like he's rowing.)

Crew Person 2: (Stops laughing) Poor guy. (Pause . . . both start laughing again.)

(Bucket of water is thrown on these two.)

Both: (Jump up and look out toward where the water came from. Say together . . .) Yuck! Whale slime!

End

Masks

Synopsis: This skit depicts how people respond to traumatic experiences and become ruled by them. Jesus shines his light on them and sees through their mask to who they really are. Jesus offers to become their hope and future if they will allow him to transform their lives through his saving grace.

Target Audience: Adult and teens. Most cultures will relate to the wearing of masks. Particularly for war-torn or third-world countries where the people are orphaned and widowed, struggle with famine, disease, and injustice.

Topic: Salvation

Cast:
Narrator: Narrator should stand offstage and translate.
Jesus: Need a good actor for this part, someone who can get across the feelings of compassion, love, and confidence. Normal clothing, but in colors of royalty or purity
Anger: Ability to look and act angry
Apathy: Ability to look and act apathetic
Unworthy: Ability to look and act rejected
Fear: Ability to look and act afraid and insecure
Lonely: Ability to look and act lonely

Props: Basket, bowl, or bag; masks. Masks should each look different. Paint them different colors or paint different expressions on them. Simple plastic masks with an elastic string purchased at a craft store will work fine.

Time: 5-15 minutes

Difficulty Level: Difficult

Customize:

1. This skit can be performed with as few as one emotion character or all five.
2. If interpreted through a translator, provide the script for the translator ahead of time. If possible, after learning the parts, practice with a translator at your last practice session.

Masks

Opening Scene: (*Characters onstage talking and walking around. All characters are wearing their masks and interacting with each other in ways typical of their emotion, except for* **Lonely,** *who is a Christian.* **Jesus** *comes onto stage wearing a sheet as a robe, carrying a basket or bag on his shoulder, and possibly holding a staff.*)

Anger: (*Should express anger by stomping feet, pushing other characters, using arms and hands expressively, crosses arms, clenches fists*)

Jesus: (*Enters stage right and stops, holds out hand*) Anger.

Anger: (*Turns around and walks over to* **Jesus** *angrily*) How did you know my name?

Jesus: I knew you when you were in your mother's womb. Why are you angry?

Anger: My brother and sister, they were murdered. My mother, died from disease. My father, gone!

Jesus: I want to help you.

Anger: Why should you want to help me? You are lying! Get away from me!

Jesus: I want to love you!

Anger: Why do you want to love me? Who are you?

Jesus: I am Jesus, the Son of the living God. I know everything about you. I know how your father treated you.

Anger: He didn't love me. I was nothing to him.

Jesus: I will be your father, your mother, your sister, your brother.

Anger: How will you do that? You're crazy!

Jesus: I can take your anger and replace it with something better.

Anger: (*Pauses thinking*) You can take away . . . my anger? You must be joking. And . . . even if you could do this, I don't know if I want to give it to you. (**Anger** *turns away from him.*)

Jesus: I know. It has become your friend. But it only leads to death. I have come that you may have life and have it abundantly.

Anger: Life? My life is gone.

Jesus:	No, your life is here, with me.
Anger:	*(Takes a step forward)* What must I do?
Jesus:	Give me your mask. I will give you my love in return. I will give you a hope and a future. I will help you to laugh again.
Anger:	Laugh? *(Puts head down thinking. Then lifts head and takes off the mask. Hands it to Jesus.)* Forgive me, Lord.
Jesus:	*(Puts the mask in the basket on his shoulders, and puts his hands on **Anger's** shoulders. Smiles)* My son *(or daughter)*, your sins are forgiven. You will now be known as "Joy."
Anger:	*(Gets down on knees and shouts, praising God and lifting hands high)* Worthy is Jesus, the Lamb of God! Worthy is the Son of the living God to be praised!

*(**Anger** stays in position during rest of skit. **Apathy** has been walking around stage and looking uninterested. Leans against something looking bored, kicks at a rock on the ground, or throws pebbles around.)*

Jesus:	*(Walks a few feet away from **Anger** and holds out hand toward **Apathy**)* Greetings, Apathy.
Apathy:	Greetings. Who are you? How do you know my name?
Jesus:	I know everything about you.
Apathy:	Why should I care? Nothing will change. Everything stays the same. I cry out for help and no one hears. No one answers.
Jesus:	I will answer.
Apathy:	What can *you* do? No one can do anything that will make a difference. My family has been scattered and torn apart.
Jesus:	I will be your family.
Apathy:	Nothing changes. The sun rises and the sun sets. Each day is the same.
Jesus:	All things are possible with God's Son, the Christ.
Apathy:	Who is this Christ? Can he make my life different? Can he stop the suffering?
Jesus:	All things work together for good for those who love him. He has come that they might have life and have it to the full.
Apathy:	How can he give this to me? I want it. Can I meet him?

Jesus:	You have met him; I am he who speaks with you.
Apathy:	*You* are the Christ! What must I do to get this full life you speak of?
Jesus:	Give me your mask. I will give you a new life.
Apathy:	My mask? *(Falls on knees, looks down)* I don't know. *(Looks up)* Can't I let you just borrow it?
Jesus:	No. You must give it to me forever.
Apathy:	*(Takes off the mask. Hands it to **Jesus**. **Jesus** puts the mask in the basket on his shoulders.)*
Jesus:	Your sins are forgiven. Now, rise my son! You will be called "Hope."
Apathy:	*(Falls down, arms outstretched to ground and praising God with shouting)* Blessed is the name of the Lord! He is the author and finisher of our faith! The Lord is a great God!

*(**Fear** has been walking around holding hands close to chest, pulling up shoulders in fear, running around stage quickly to get away from the others, going to edges of stage and trying to hide. **Jesus** walks a few feet and holds out hand towards **Fear**.)*

Jesus:	Fear, I want to speak with you.
Fear:	*(Looks around fearfully, then slowly walks up to **Jesus**)* Did you call to me?
Jesus:	Yes. Your name is Fear.
Fear:	How do you know my name?
Jesus:	You do not need to fear any longer. I am here.
Fear:	*(Acts worried)* Who are you? How do you know my name?
Jesus:	You were taken captive. You were beaten. You were abandoned. You have seen much death.
Fear:	*(Very anxious now)* How do you know these things? What are you going to do to me? Please don't hurt me!
Jesus:	I love you.
Fear:	No! It's a trick! You don't love me! No one really loves me!
Jesus:	I have been calling to you since you were born.
Fear:	I didn't hear you.

Jesus: You weren't listening. I have always been with you.

Fear: (Upset) But I was so alone in the dark. I was so scared. Where were you?

Jesus: Right beside you. Waiting for you to hear and to see. Let me love you.

Fear: I am afraid! I'm afraid you will hurt me. You will leave me.

Jesus: There now child, I will be a Father to you. I will give you peace and rest even in the middle of the storm. When others around you are frightened, I will give you calm. When you are in the dark, I will give you light.

Fear: I want this so much. What must I do?

Jesus: Believe in me. Give me your mask. I will be with you forever. You will never have to fear again.

Fear: (Takes off the mask. Hands it to **Jesus**. **Jesus** puts the mask in the basket on his shoulders.)

Jesus: (Holds **Fear's** shoulders) Your sins are forgiven. You will now be called "Courage."

Fear: (Falls down, arms raised high and praises God with shouting) Worthy is the Lamb! Worthy is the King of Kings and Lord of Lords!

Unworthy: (Walks around stage with shoulders slumped, head down, bumps into people then walks quickly aside, gets pushed by **Anger** and does nothing, walks to edge of stage—away from **Fear**—and holds head in face)

Jesus: (Walks a few feet and holds out hand)

Jesus: Unworthy.

Unworthy: (Stands far away, looks sideways to **Jesus**) Yes? Are you calling to me?

Jesus: Come to me.

Unworthy: (Looks away again) I am not worthy to talk to you kind sir. Why talk to me? I am nothing.

Jesus: You were created in God's image.

Unworthy: You don't understand. I am not good at anything. I can't do anything right.

Jesus: I have a plan and a purpose for you.

Unworthy: I am unwanted, unloved.

Jesus: I love you. I have chosen you and appointed you to go and bear fruit.

Unworthy: Chosen me? I am a burden to others.

Jesus: Call unto me in the wilderness, and I will deliver you from your distress.

Unworthy: I am nothing.

Jesus: You are created to be holy.

Unworthy: But I am not. I am dirty and unholy.

Jesus: I will make you clean. You will wear the garment of salvation.

Unworthy: Lord, *(Turns and rushes over to him)* how may I come to be clean?

Jesus: Believe in me. Follow me. Give up your mask.

Unworthy: *(Takes off the mask. Hands it to **Jesus**. **Jesus** puts the mask in the basket on his shoulders.)*

Jesus: *(Holds **Unworthy's** shoulders)* Your sins are forgiven. I have given you a crown of beauty instead of ashes. You will now be called "Righteous."

Unworthy: *(Falls down, arms outstretched to ground and praises God)* You are worthy to be praised! Shout for joy to the Lord, all the earth!

Lonely: *(A Christian—walks around the outside of the stage circling everyone else, doesn't see others, stops and leans face on hand and arm, keeps looking away as **Jesus** talks with him.)*

Jesus: *(Walks a few more feet and holds out hand)*

Jesus: Lonely.

Lonely: Yes Lord.

Jesus: I am calling to you.

Lonely: Lord, I am lost and alone.

Jesus: Remember what I said? I will never leave you nor forsake you.

Lonely: I believe in you, Lord, and you have forgiven my sins, but I don't feel your presence.

Jesus: You have forgotten my goodness and faithfulness.

Lonely: You allowed my family and friends to leave me. Everyone is gone now.

Jesus: I am still here. I have never left you.

Lonely: Why don't I hear you?

Jesus: You have forgotten how to listen.

Lonely: Can I see you? Can I touch you?

Jesus: Whenever you help the lowliest people, you are helping me.

Lonely: I do not help the lowliest, Lord.

Jesus: Let me help you. I have loved you with an everlasting love; I have drawn you with loving kindness.

Lonely: *(Turns to **Jesus** now)* What must I do?

Jesus: You are to love one another, for love comes from God.

Lonely: *(Walks over to him)* Yes, Lord.

Jesus: Give to those who have need; I will make your righteousness shine like stars. I will give you grace and glory; no good thing will I withhold from you.

Lonely: *(Walks over to **Jesus** and kneels down)*

Jesus: *(Puts a white robe over **Lonely's** shoulders)* I will give you the garment of praise. You will now be called "Thankful."

Lonely: *(Stands with arms outstretched and praises God with shouting)* Thanks be to God! The author and the finisher of my faith! He is my rock and my salvation! I will forever trust in the name of the Lord!

End

All Heart (a mime)

Synopsis: This mime shows people in sin, and Jesus asks for their heart. Some say no, but when a women testifies to her changed life, they say yes.

Target Audience: Adults and teens. Buddhists, Muslims, Jews, Hindus, Taoists, and Celts see the heart symbol as something positive.

Topics: Salvation, Addiction, Forgiveness

Cast:

Jesus: Wears a robe and sash

Drunk: Scruffy looking man, sloppily dressed (If doing this in an urban area, have him dressed as a businessman. If not, then have him dress as someone from a rural area.)

Rich Man: Dressed as someone with a lot of money for the region

Abusive Woman: Should be dressed like a mom of a teen girl

Daughter: Dressed like a normal teen

Props: Wallet, play money, four black paper hearts, four white paper hearts, bottle in a paper bag

Time: 5 minutes

Difficulty Level: Easy

Customize: Add extra people to the scene: people for the drunk to drink with, a bartender, businessmen who talk with the rich man (or a butler or servant who attends to the rich man), or siblings of the daughter.

All Heart (a mime)

Opening Scene: *(Characters are on the stage. **Drunk** is stage left, **Rich Man** is upstage center and **Abusive Woman** and **Daughter** are stage right. **Jesus** enters from stage left. Everyone should have a large black paper heart taped to the front of their shirt. Tape four white hearts on top of each other on the front of Jesus' shirt.)*

Narrator:	(Holds up paper heart) The heart. Throughout the centuries and across cultures, it is a powerful symbol. It represents the three elements of the soul—the mind. The will. The emotions.
Jesus:	*(Walks up to **Drunk**. **Jesus** points to his own heart and gestures for **Drunk** to give him his heart.)*
Drunk:	*(He looks down, lifts up his bottle, takes a drink, and offers his drink to **Jesus**.)*
Jesus:	*(Shakes his head no, then gestures for the man's heart again.)*
Drunk:	*(He cups both hands together at his heart, brings them down, and looks at his "heart" in his hands. He looks at **Jesus**.)*
Jesus:	*(Holds out his hand for the man's heart.)*
Drunk:	*(Puts his heart back, picks up his bottle and looks at it. Takes a drink, wipes his mouth and puts the bottle down. **Drunk** shakes his head while looking down, then he turns his back on **Jesus**, grabs his bottle, and walks two steps away, takes a drink.)*
Jesus:	*(Turns and walks up to **Rich Man**. **Jesus** points to his own heart and gestures for **Rich Man** to give him his heart.)*
Rich Man:	*(He cups both hands together at his heart, brings them down, and looks at his "heart" in his hands. He looks at **Jesus**. Shakes his head, puts his heart back, grabs his wallet, and counts his money. He offers **Jesus** a few bills.)*
Jesus:	*(Doesn't take the bills.)*
Rich Man:	*(Holds his wallet tightly to his heart with both hands and shrugs his shoulders. He takes a step and walks past **Jesus** a few steps toward stage left. Stops and counts his money again.)*
Jesus:	*(Walks up to the **Abusive Woman**)*

Abusive Woman:	(Doesn't notice **Jesus** and starts waving her arms angrily at her **Daughter**)
Daughter:	(Stands with head down looking afraid the whole time)
Jesus:	(Touches **Abusive Woman's** arm lightly)
Abusive Woman:	(Jumps when **Jesus** touches her, turns, and looks into his face. Then she looks down.)
Jesus:	(He lifts her chin. **Jesus** points to his own heart and gestures for **Abusive Woman** to give him her heart.)
Abusive Woman:	(Puts her hands on her heart and looks down sadly)
Jesus:	(Lifts her chin again, then holds out his hands to receive her heart)
Abusive Woman:	(Looks at her **Daughter**, then looks at **Jesus**. She holds out her hands with her heart to give to **Jesus**.)
Jesus:	(Takes her heart with one hand and smiles widely at her. He puts his other hand on his own heart and gives it to her. Removes one white heart and hands it to **Woman**)
Abusive Woman:	(She receives it with both hands and places it back where her heart was. She smiles, and they both start to laugh. She grabs her **Daughter** who looks worriedly at her, but she hugs her and then holds her face in her hands lovingly. She gestures for her **Daughter** to give **Jesus** her heart, and her **Daughter** gives him her heart willingly, with Jesus giving her a white heart in exchange. They all hug.)
Abusive Woman:	(Walks up to **Drunk** and gestures toward her **Daughter**, gestures toward heaven, puts hands on her heart. She points toward the bottle. She is very happy. **Daughter** standing stage right is very happy.)
Drunk:	(Gets down on knees and holds heart up to **Jesus**, who trades him for a white heart. **Drunk** jumps up, throws away bottle, and dances around.)
Abusive Woman: Drunk, and Daughter:	(Run up to **Rich Man**. Loving **Woman** gestures toward her **Daughter**, then toward **Drunk**. She gestures toward heaven and puts hands on her heart. She points toward the **Man's** wallet. All three are very happy.)

Rich Man: (Takes his wallet and counts his money. Walks away and suddenly has a heart attack, falls over dead.)

Abusive Woman, Drunk, and Daughter: (Run over to him and check for a pulse. They look enquiringly at *Jesus*, who shakes his head in sadness and walks off stage. All exit.)

Narrator: Your heart. It is yours to give. It is yours to keep. It is yours to trade. God's word says, "For this people's heart has become calloused; they hardly hear with their ears, and they have closed their eyes. Otherwise they might see with their eyes, hear with their ears, understand with their hearts and turn, and I would heal them." (Acts 28:27).

End

A Tree (a mime)

Synopsis: Husband is a drunk and hangs around a tree. Wife brings first fruits to tree. They bring their sick friend to the witch doctor to be healed, but he dies.

Target Audience: Adults and teens. Directed toward people who practice primitive religions (i.e., animism, witchcraft, and voodoo) who often leave food sacrifices to particular trees believed to have spirits. People in various areas of Europe also take part in these practices.

Topics: Idolatry, Marriage

Cast:

Husband: Easy part to play. It would be good to dress in typical dress of region.

Wife: Easy part to play. It would be good to dress in typical dress of region.

Pastor: Easy part to play. It would be good to dress in typical dress of region.

Tree: Should be a guy dressed all in green. Gloves and makeup of same color would strengthen the idea that this is a tree.

Demons: Two or three actors, dressed in all black

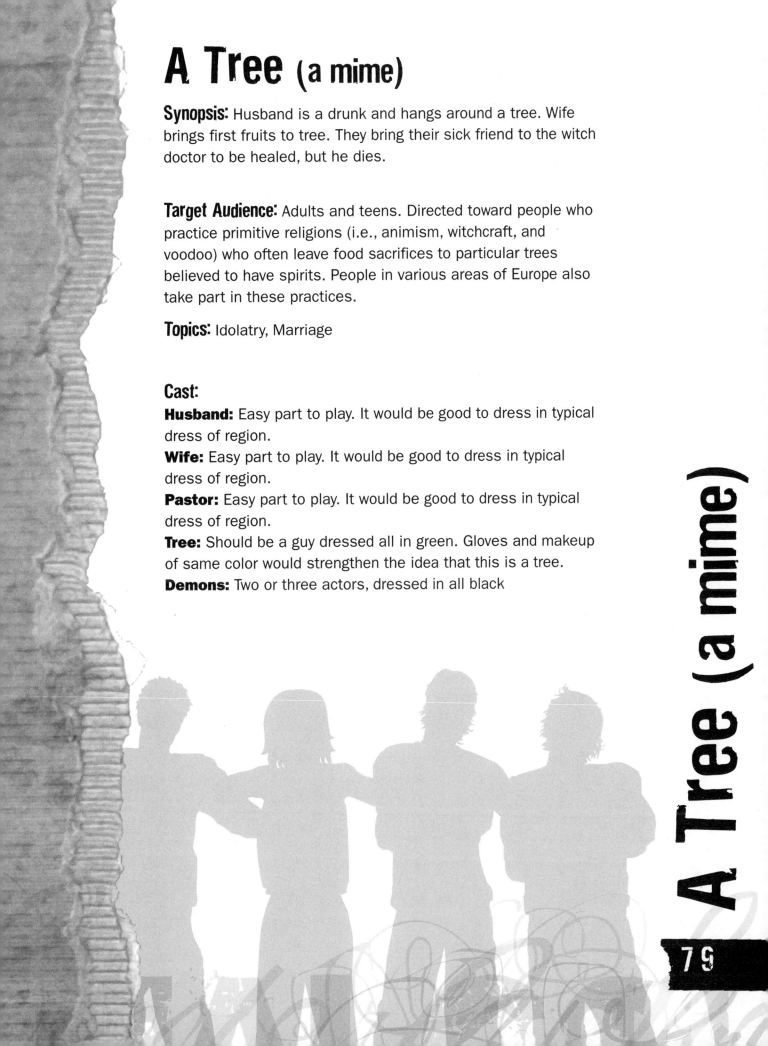

Props: Bowl of fruit, machete, shovel, empty liquor bottle (or bottle in a paper bag). Optional: gloves and makeup for demons and tree, Bible

Time: 5 minutes

Difficulty Level: Easy

Customize: For English-speaking people, change this from a mime to a script by adding in lines for each character.

A Tree (a mime)

Opening Scene: (*Tree is standing downstage center with arms bent.*)

Husband: (*Enters stage left. He is drunk and walks unevenly toward the Tree. He starts to dance around the Tree.*)

Wife: (*Walks on from stage right. Husband gestures for Wife to come over to the Tree. She places bowl of fruit before the Tree, and they both bow low before it.*)

Demons: (*Enter stage left. Hover around Tree and people. Run in between Husband and Wife.*)

(*Note: Throughout skit, Demons need to be obviously influencing the Husband and Wife. They are pointing at her and tempting him to drink and hit her.*)

Wife: (*Looks angrily at her Husband with hands on hips. Points toward stage right.*)

Husband: (*Waves his bottle at her and dismisses her. Pours drink down his throat and plops down next to Tree. Pats Tree.*)

Wife: (*Walks over to Husband and grabs his bottle, throwing it away.*)

Demons: (*Laughing and clapping*)

Husband: (*Jumps up and grabs his Wife's arm, (fake) strikes her*)

Wife: (*Falls down crying with head in hand*)

Demons: (*Laughing and pointing at Wife*)

Pastor: (*Enters stage right with a machete*)

Demons: (*Run to other side of stage and hide, watching*)

Husband: (*Stands up and stumbles across stage, walking offstage left*)

Pastor: (*Starts to chop at tree roots with his machete*)

Wife: (*Turns around and watches*)

Pastor: (*Is now using shovel to dig at roots*)

Husband: (*Comes back from stage left. Stumbles over to Pastor and tries to take shovel*)

Pastor: (*Puts his arm around the Husband. He gestures toward his Wife.*)

Wife:	*(Stands up and walks over tentatively)*
Pastor:	*(Picks up his Bible and starts to read from it)*
Husband:	*(Takes **Wife's** hand. They stare at one another.)*
Pastor:	*(Picks up machete and continues to chop at the roots)*
Husband and Wife:	*(Join him in tearing down the tree, pushing and pulling at branches.)*
Demons:	*(Are mad, stomping up and down with hands clenched)*
All Three:	*(Push down **Tree**)*
Demons:	*(Run away, screaming out loud)*
Pastor, Husband, and Wife:	*(Hold hands in prayer)*
Pastor:	*(Out loud)* Lord, thank you for this couple, who you want to love each other. Thank you for Jesus, who can give the deepest kind of peace. Thank you for restoring this man and woman to each other.
All three:	*(Sit down)*
Pastor:	*(Takes out Bible and reads to **Husband** and **Wife**.)* The book of John: the beginning of the gospel of Jesus Christ, the Son of God . . .

End

The Created: Part 1—Fall

(a narrated choreography)

Synopsis: This is the creation story told as a mime—great performed for street evangelism. The colored cloth will attract attention as it adds excitement and movement to the mime and aids the element of time. This skit should not be stagnant but have constant movement. Narration and action should happen simultaneously.

Target Audience: Buddhists, Shintoists, Jews, and Muslims. Eastern cultures aren't familiar with the creation story of a God who created everything. Jews and Muslims believe in God, the creator, so will be pulled into the story line that finishes with the death and resurrection of Christ.

Topics: Creation, Sin

Cast:

Adam: Dressed in matching tan shirt and pants

Eve: Dressed in matching tan shirt and pants

Deceiver: Dressed in all black

Trees: At least three. Dressed in green and brown

Colors: There are two people per cloth color. They should dress either in all white or the same color as the cloths. The two people should hold each end of the nine-foot length of cloth stretched out to its full length, so it ripples and waves between them. This is meant to be a graceful and energetic effect. The cloth should be extended out to its full length whenever possible. Cloth enters and exits *as* narrator speaks, not after.

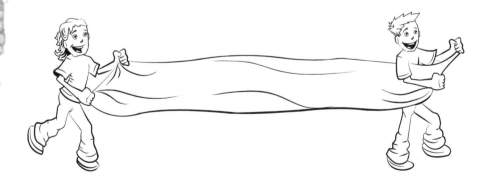

Animals: Choose any animals you want, and have the characters dress in the color of the animal (i.e., gray shirt and pants for an elephant).

Props: Three-yard lengths (45-inch-wide bolts) of solid colored cloth—light blue, red, brown, white, and black cloth. (Buy fabric that moves easily, like rayon. Many fabric stores have remnant tables with inexpensive prices. You can also buy white fabric and dye it the colors you will need.)

Time: 10 minutes

Difficulty Level: Difficult, due to synchronizing of cloth and movement

Customize:

1. To add an element of dance, choose people who have experience in dance to hold cloth. Allow them to wear ballet shoes and run or walk in form. Consider using drums or Djembe to add drama and rhythm.
2. Turn the entire mime into a dance. All characters should have ballet experience or be trained in simple movements. Choose dramatic music for the dance. Remember to bring a portable stereo and mike for street evangelism.
3. Make costumes for everyone in the performance.

The Created: Part 1—Fall (a narrated choreography)

Opening Scene: *(An empty stage.)*

Narrator: In the beginning, God created the heavens and the earth. God said "Let there be light," and he separated the light from the dark.

*(**Black Cloth** and **White Cloth** enter from opposite ends of the stage. When the **Narrator** says "Let there be Light," **Black Cloth** gets lowered toward the ground, and **White Cloth** gets raised toward the sky. Then the two colors run off opposite ends of stage.)*

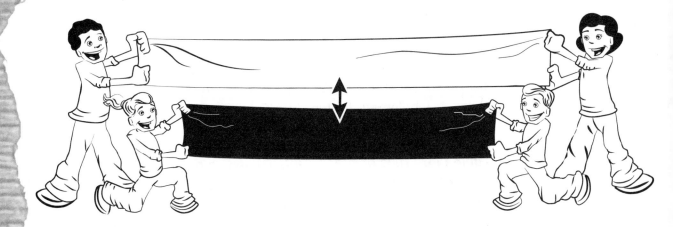

Narrator: God gathered the waters and formed the sky and let dry ground appear, and it was so.

*(**Blue Cloth** runs on from stage left, and **Brown Cloth** runs on from stage right. Lower **Brown Cloth** toward ground and **Blue Cloth** toward sky. Then the two colors run off opposite ends of stage.)*

Narrator: Then God created the plants; he separated night and day; and he created the birds, the fish, and the animals.

*(Various **Animals** enter stage right and left. Each **Animal** should act out its characteristics with sound. Come onto stage, wander or run around, and wander offstage opposite.)*

*(While the **Animals** are walking around the stage, **Adam** enters from stage left, hidden behind **Brown Cloth**. He stops upstage center and lies down. **Brown Cloth** then lies flat over him, covering him up. The two people holding cloth should stay in position as **Animals** exit stage.)*

Narrator: Then God formed man from the dust of the ground and breathed into his nostrils the breath of life, and man became a living being.

*(The two people holding **Brown Cloth** shake it close to the ground to create waving motion. As **Adam** is lying beneath the cloth, he starts to rise up while still under cloth, then comes up out of cloth. He stands up. The two people holding the cloth stay crouched down and let cloth fall to the floor.)*

Narrator: God planted the very first garden on the earth, in the East, called Eden. God told Adam, "You can eat from any tree in the garden, except one. From it you must not eat or you will die."

*(**Trees** come onto stage slowly facing audience, arms extended up like tree branches. One **Tree** stays separate from the rest. **Adam** walks over to a normal **Tree**, picks fruit, and eats it. Then he sits down, looking lonely.)*

Narrator: God said, "It is not good for man to be alone. I will create a helpmate for him." So God created a woman from the rib of **Adam**. **Adam** called her **Eve**.

*(**Blue Cloth** runs on stage right, hiding **Eve** behind them. They encircle **Adam**. **Blue Cloth** is shaken and then moves away from **Adam** and **Eve** and exits stage left with **Brown Cloth**. **Adam** and **Eve** are left standing and looking at each other, holding hands. They walk over and pick fruit from a normal **Tree**.)*

Narrator: A Deceiver in the garden said to Eve, "God told you not to eat from *that* tree because he doesn't want you to be like him."

*(**Deceiver** enters stage left, waves arms, and gestures toward the lone **Tree**. Walks quickly all around **Adam**, **Eve**, and the **Tree** gesturing with his arms and bending over slightly, exaggerating movements. Goes behind the **Tree** and gestures for **Eve** to come over)*

Narrator: Eve was tempted by the Deceiver, ate the forbidden fruit, and gave some to Adam. The fruit gave them knowledge of good and evil. Then they were afraid and hid from God.

*(**Eve** walks over and eats fruit from the **Tree**. She gestures to **Adam** to come over and eat. **Adam** eats fruit from **Eve**. Once they've eaten, they react violently, throw up arms, drop their fruit, and hide behind **Tree** looking ashamed.)*

Narrator: God saw Adam and Eve's shame and cursed the Deceiver. God sent Adam and Eve out of the garden to labor and work hard. As a result of eating the fruit, Adam and Eve—and all mankind—would some-day die and return to the ground from which they came.

(**Adam** stands up and looks offstage. Points toward **Eve**. **Eve** points toward the **Deceiver**. **Deceiver** backs away and falls to the ground in fear. Slinks away along ground off stage right. **Red Cloth** enters stage left, covers **Adam** and **Eve**, and all exit stage left.)

Optional: (Intermission with a testimony or short message here)

The Created: Part 2—Redemption

Synopsis: *Redemption* is the second part of *Fall*. Man continues in sin on the earth. Jesus dies on the cross and is resurrected, bringing salvation.

Target Audience: Adults, youth, children, Buddhists, Shintoists, Jews, and Muslims. Eastern cultures aren't familiar with the creation story of a God who created everything. Jews and Muslims believe in God, the creator, so will be pulled into the story line that finishes with the death and resurrection of Christ.

Topics: Sin, Salvation

Cast:
Adam: Dressed in matching tan shirt and pants, now wrapped in black cloth, symbolizing clothes and sin
Eve: Dressed in matching tan shirt and pants, now wrapped in black cloth, symbolizing clothes and sin
Colors: Same as in *The Created: Part 1*
Jesus: Dressed in white
Soldiers: At least two people, dressed in anything military looking
Violence: Three men who are fighting. One gets killed.
Disease: One person who is sick. Use makeup to create spots or unsightly skin.
Famine: Two people who are hungry

Props: See *The Created: Part 1*. Large hand bell

Time: 10 minutes

Difficulty Level: Difficult, due to synchronizing of cloth and movement

Customize: See the Customize notes for *The Created: Part 1*

The Created: Part 2—Redemption

Opening Scene: (*Adam* and *Eve* are standing stage left in the Garden of Eden, which is filled with *Trees*. [See end of The Created: Part 1.]

(*Adam* and *Eve* cross right, stop and look back at the garden with longing, waving goodbye. *Adam*, *Eve*, and *Trees* walk offstage right.)

Narrator: Because of Adam and Eve's disobedience to God, sin entered men's hearts. Murder plagued mankind.

(*Violence* actors enter stage left pushing each other and fighting. Two of them stab the other, killing him. He falls to the ground. They freeze leaning over the dead man. *Red Cloth* enters stage left and swirls around *Violence*. *Red Cloth* exits stage right.)

Narrator: Disease plagues mankind.

(*Disease* enters stage right, slumps over, and is barely able to walk. Lies down, downstage center. Freezes. *Black Cloth* runs on stage right and swirls around *Disease*. *Black Cloth* exits stage left.)

Narrator: And Famine plagued mankind.

(*Famine* actors, one holding an empty basket, walk slowly onstage left, holding stomachs in pain. They sit down together and turn the basket upside down to show it's empty. They put their heads down. Freeze. *Brown Cloth* enters stage left and swirls around *Famine*. *Brown Cloth* exits stage right.)

Narrator: God still loved the people he created and wanted to help them avoid the consequences of murder and disease, so he set up laws for men to follow. But man broke even those laws, so God sent his Son, Jesus, to make a way through the despair of man's lawlessness.

(*Jesus* enters stage right and walks up to *Disease*. He holds out his hand. *Disease* takes Jesus' hand and rises to her feet. She acts very happy and runs off stage right to tell others the news.)

Narrator: He fed the hungry.

(*Jesus* walks up to *Famine* actors and takes their empty basket and gives them food to eat. They eat the food, then bow down to *Jesus*. *Famine* actors are very happy and run off stage left to tell others the news.)

Narrator: He brought the dead to life.

(Jesus walks up to two people who have killed their friend. They look frightened and back away as Jesus approaches. Jesus walks up to the dead Violence actor and holds out arms, looking at heaven. Actor begins to rise as he comes to life. He feels where his wound was and looks at his two companions.)

Narrator: He forgave men for breaking God's laws.

(The two other Violence actors take a step back. Then they run over to Jesus and fall at his knees bowing low. Jesus places a hand on each head, and they stand up. The third actor walks over and hugs his enemies. They all walk off stage right.)

Narrator: Jesus brought healing both to body and soul, bridging the gap between man and God.

(Jesus stands upstage center and raises his hands to heaven while closing his eyes.)

Narrator: But there were many who did not accept this teaching and had Jesus arrested. Jesus, God's Son, was scourged nearly to death, then nailed to a cross, and hung to die.

(Soldiers march onto stage. They take Jesus by the arms, tie a rope on his hands, and lead him to stand stage right. Jesus is forced to his knees, hands tied in front while soldiers act like they are beating him. They untie his hands and hold them straight out, hammering one hand at a time. Jesus hangs his head.)

Narrator: Jesus died on the cross, and the people mourned for him. They took him and buried him in a tomb.

(Red Cloth runs onstage left over to Jesus, running around stage while Narrator speaks. Stops and lifts Red Cloth so it covers and drapes completely over Jesus. Let go of it and bow heads backing away to run offstage right. Disease, Famine, and Violence come onto stage one at a time to mourn Jesus' death. They "take him down" and carry him to upstage center, laying him down. Red Cloth people enter stage right, take away the cloth, run offstage left. White Cloth runs onstage right and drapes over Jesus. White Cloth people leave cloth and run offstage left. All people onstage back away from Jesus and move backwards offstage both left and right or turn at the end and walk off. Large hand bell rings three times slowly.)

Narrator: But death, where is your sting? Jesus is God's Son . . . after three days he rose from the dead. He has conquered the grave!

(Jesus moves from under the White Cloth and stands up. He leaves the cloth and walks off stage left.)

(**Famine** actors walk onstage right very slowly and mournfully, holding each other's arms. One runs over and picks up the **White Cloth** holding it up for the other to see. **Jesus** enters stage left and walks up to them. They run up to **Jesus** and jump for joy. All other people run onto stage from all directions praising God and rejoicing, dancing.)

Narrator: Jesus will take your sin and give you a new life if you ask him.

(All **Colored Cloths** enter stage from both directions. Create waving up and down and circle around while **Jesus** walks to downstage center and holds out his hands to the audience.)

End

Leading the Way

Synopsis: Gets across the idea of many people going the wrong way in life, the way that leads to death. One person is walking toward life and tries to share the news with others.

Target Audience: Adults and teens. The language of a path and door are common to the religions of Buddhists, Hindus, Shintoists, and Toaists.

Topic: Seeking God

Cast:

Crowd: Get as many people as you can to take part in this. You could even ask youth from the indigenous church to take part as extras. The idea to get across is a very large crowd walking through life. Children and adults can be included.

Christian: A good actor. Wears everyday clothes

Teen Girl: A good actor. Normal teen clothes

Young Man: Everyday clothes, collared shirt

Old Woman: White or gray hair, dress with sweater, large purse, cane or walking stick (find a branch to use rather than bringing a cane)

Businessman: Nice clothes, collared shirt, suit coat. Carrying a nice bag or briefcase

Teen Boy: Normal teen clothes

Props: None

Time: 3 minutes

Difficulty Level: Easy

Customize:

1. Turn this into a mime. Use exaggerated gestures while talking with people and trying to show them the right way. Make a large sign to hold up at the end that says, "Wide is the gate and broad is the road that leads to destruction, and many enter through it. But small is the gate and narrow the road that leads to life, and only a few find it" (Matt. 7:13-14).

2. While in the field, observe the indigenous people around you, and gather props to mimic the culture. (e.g., Have someone ride by on a bike, others carry food on their heads, kids carry school books.)

3. For a performance at your home church, make this relevant for your audience. If performing before youth, have a lot of teens in the crowd and provide props and clothing so there are a variety of people in the crowd. Instead of an old woman, make her character a teen girl. Change her dialogue appropriately.

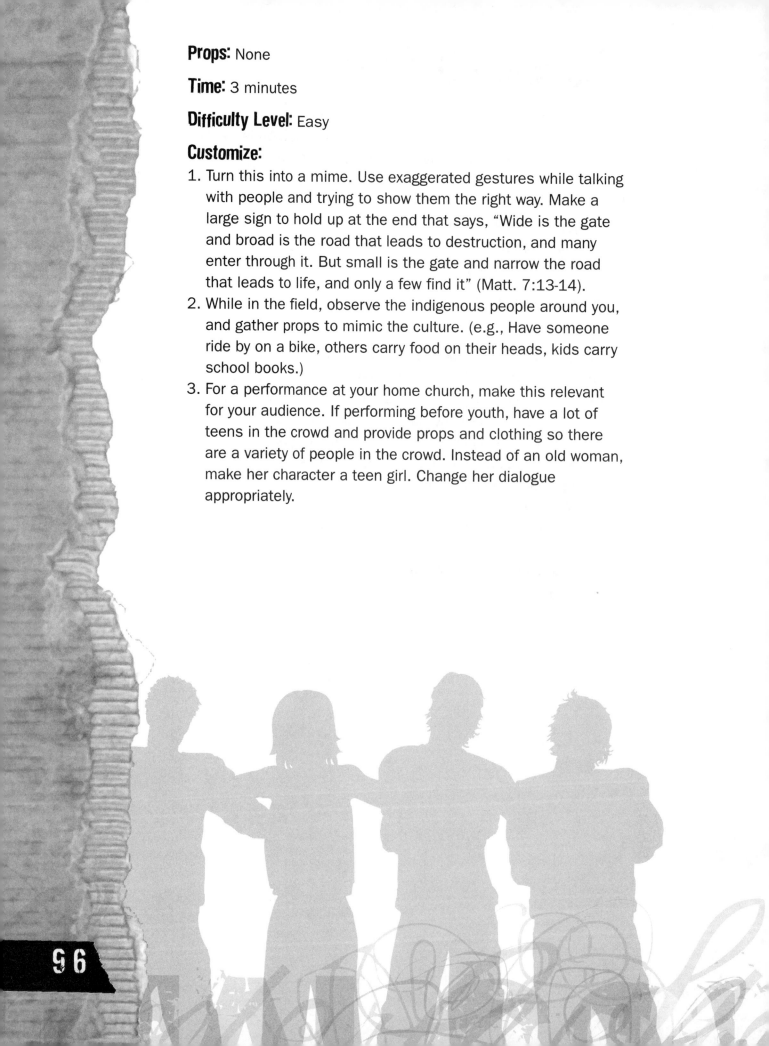

Leading the Way

Opening Scene: (**Crowd** grouped together, starts to walk across the stage from stage left going the same direction . . . toward stage right. **Crowd** walks in a large circle around stage edge to give the impression of continuous movement. **Christian** walks from stage right toward the crowd.)

Christian:	(Stops **Young Man**)

(**Crowd** freezes.)

Christian:	Excuse me, where are you going?
Young Man:	I'm following them. (Points at the people ahead of him.)
Christian:	(Turns and looks at them) Where are they going?
Young Man:	They're looking for enlightenment.
Christian:	How do you know it's in that direction?
Young Man:	Because they are going that way. (**Young Man** and **Crowd** start to walk again.)
Christian:	(Takes a couple steps to **Old Woman**) Where are you going?

(**Crowd** freezes.)

Old Woman:	(Points) That way.
Christian:	Is that the right way?
Old Woman:	I'm not sure, but it's the way I've been walking all these long years, and I'm going to keep walking this way.
Christian:	But what if it's the wrong way?
Old Woman:	Well, I'll take my chances. My husband walked this way, and so will I. (She and **Crowd** start to walk again.)
Christian:	(Takes a few steps and stops in front of **Businessman**) Why are you going this way?

(**Crowd** freezes.)

Businessman:	I can't talk to you. I'm in too much of a hurry! (Starts to walk past him)
Christian:	But, wait! (**Businessman** stops.) You are going the wrong way!

Businessman: What does it matter which way I go? All roads lead to the same place. (**Businessman** and **Crowd** start to walk again.)

Christian: (Walks in front of **Teen Girl**) Do you know where you are going?

(**Crowd** freezes.)

Teen Girl: No! I've been searching for the right way. Everyone is going this way, but somehow I feel it isn't the right way.

Christian: You're right! That is the way that leads to death!

Teen Girl: It is? But which way leads to life?

Christian: If you turn around and walk the other way, you will walk toward life.

Teen Girl: But the others are all walking toward death. (She looks around at the others.)

Christian: Yes. In the Bible, God says, "Wide is the gate and broad is the road that leads to destruction, and many enter through it. But small is the gate and narrow the road that leads to life, and only a few find it."

Teen Girl: (Turns around and looks the opposite way) All I have to do is turn around?

Christian: Yes, that's the right path to the gate of life; just walk toward it.

Teen Girl: I believe you. (She turns around and starts walking.)

(Everyone starts walking again. **Teen Girl** stops in front of a **Teen Boy**.)

Teen Girl: Where are you going?

(The rest of the **Crowd** walks off stage, leaving **Christian**, **Teen Girl**, and **Teen Boy** alone on stage.)

End

To Wait or Not to Wait?

Synopsis: People are waiting in line to get into heaven. Man gets in line for heaven but then decides to get in line for hell because it seems to have a better offer.

Target Audience: Adults and youth. Any culture.

Topics: Heaven and Hell, Choices

Cast:
Hurried Man: Actor who can speak very loudly and exaggerate feelings
Patient Man: Gives an air of confidence, waiting patiently, answers in a matter-of-fact way, good-natured.
Waiting Woman: Eager to get through the line
People in Line: Try to have enough people for a long line across the stage

Props: Two wristwatches, brochure

Time: 5 minutes

Difficulty Level: Easy

Customize:
1. Have young and old people in the line wearing all different types of clothing, dressed in the style of clothing of the culture you are visiting.
2. Have people in line dressed in clothing representing different tribes and nations from around the world.

To Wait or Not to Wait?

Opening Scene: *(Many people lined up for entrance to some place. Line begins somewhere offstage.)*

Hurried Man: *(Runs up and stands behind **Patient Man**. Anxiously steps from foot to foot looking around the man in front of him. Taps man on shoulder)* Hey, how long have you been in line?

Patient Man: *(Looks at his watch)* About an hour.

Hurried Man: Are you kidding me? I'm going to miss my flight!

Patient Man: What time does it leave?

Hurried Man: *(Looks perplexed. Pats his pockets.)* I don't know; I lost my ticket.

Patient Man: I'm sorry to hear that! I hope they can help you.

Hurried Man: *(Looks at his watch, walks slightly out of line and back, paces. Finally leans over and yells)* Hey, what's the holdup??

Waiting Woman: Shh, they're helping someone else right now. You have to be patient.

Hurried Man: *(Says to **Patient Man**)* How do you like that? She says I have to be patient!

Patient Man: I heard they can only help one person at a time.

Hurried Man: Why? They should open up another line!

Patient Man: I also heard there's another line somewhere. But I don't know its destination.

Hurried Man: Really? Maybe I should go and look for it!

Patient Man: Are you sure you want to? This plane takes you to a great place! Have you seen the brochure? *(Holds brochure out for man to see)*

Hurried Man: Let me see that. Hmm, n-i-c-e! This place is beautiful! Crystal clear water . . . must be some great snorkeling!

Patient Man: *(Leans over and points to the brochure)* It's all-inclusive, too.

Hurried Man: The food in the photos looks good. I don't know. *(Hands back the brochure)* But I'm in such a hurry! I think I might try out the other line instead.

Patient Man: But that line could be twice as long as this one!

(Offstage a voice calls out "N-e-x-t!")

Hurried Man: We're finally moving!

Patient Man: *(Laughs good-naturedly)* Don't get too excited. Sometimes they take awhile!

Hurried Man: Why don't they work faster? Who's in charge around here? Why are they so slow?

Patient Man: I've seen the manager come around from time to time. He likes to make sure the travel package you booked is just right.

Hurried Man: *(Still pacing and bouncing from one foot to the next)* Well, next time you see him, call him over here! I want to talk to him! I'm starving!

Patient Man: They say you can get fast food while you wait in that other line.

Hurried Man: Really? That sounds pretty good.

Patient Man: I also heard there are constant commercials to keep you distracted while you wait, but who knows if it's true.

Hurried Man: Food? Entertainment?! What else does this other line offer?

Patient Man: Well, they offer worldly success, lots of money, but hey . . . you're not thinking of switching lines are you? You'll lose your spot! Stay here with us. We can stick it out together. *(Slaps his hand on the guy's back.)* Don't forget about this great brochure! *(Shows him the brochure again.)*

Hurried Man: *(Pushes his hand away)* But I could go over there, get food and entertainment, right now!

Patient Man: Well, that is *if* it's all true! It's just rumors you know. I wouldn't, if I were you!

Hurried Man: I'm in too much of a hurry to wait here any longer. I have a life to live you know! *(Hurried man rushes offstage left)*

Waiting Woman: *(Turns and says to **Patient Man**)* Did he say *life*?

Patient Man: *(Looks where **Hurried Man** exited)* Yeah, he's pretty confused, isn't he? I think he was in the wrong line.

Waiting Woman: Do you think he'll try to come back?

Patient Man: No. That other line is too glitzy, even if the destination is no good.

Waiting Woman: So sorry for him. *(Pulls out her brochure and opens it)* I can't believe how amazing this will be. *(Looks around people toward the front)* Heaven will be wonderful!

End

The Gift

Synopsis: A man offers a gift (the free gift of salvation) and is turned down.

Target Audience: Any

Topic: Salvation

Cast:
Merchant: Loud, outgoing, no-nonsense type
Gift Giver: Nicely dressed, upbeat
Customers: Different ages, walking by and checking out Merchant's shirts for sale

Time: 3 minutes

Props: Three shirts, a small wrapped gift

Difficulty Level: Easy

Customize:
As it is, this is a simple, easy-to-do-anywhere skit. But if you have two particularly gifted actors, you can expand the back story of the Merchant, and the motivation of the Gift Giver. Make up other things the Merchant is in bondage to (addictions, unhealthy relationships), which he and the Gift Giver can discuss. Also, have the characters talk about the reason the Gift Giver is offering something for nothing (he cares about the Merchant, his gift is so valuable that no price would be enough).

The Gift

Opening Scene: (**Merchant** *is standing downstage center selling shirts on a street. Lays shirts out on the ground. Holds one or two shirts in hand.*)

Merchant: Sh-i-rts! New shirts for sale!

Gift Giver: *(Approaches from stage right)*

Merchant: Would you like to buy a new shirt?

Gift Giver: No, are you <u>Brandon Smith</u>? *[Choose a name that is indigenous to the region.]*

Merchant: Yes, who are you?

Gift Giver: I have a gift for you.

Merchant: A gift? What's the catch?

Gift Giver: There is no catch. It's a free gift.

Merchant: Nothing is for free! What are you selling?

Gift Giver: I'm not selling anything. I simply want to give you a gift.

Merchant: What do you want in return then?

Gift Giver: Nothing at all. It's a free gift for you, Brandon. All you have to do is accept it.

Merchant: Well, if that's true, how about if you give me the gift, I'll give you a shirt in return.

Gift Giver: No, I don't want anything in return. But there is one thing you have to do.

Merchant: I knew it!

Gift Giver: You have to turn your life over to me.

Merchant: Tell me one good reason I should turn my life over to you! I don't even know you!

Gift Giver: I can set you free.

Merchant: Free? I am free. Do you see me standing here in chains?

Gift Giver: Actually, yes I do. Can I take you out to lunch?

Merchant: Oh, no! I don't have time for lunch; I've gotta make my quota. I'm not my own boss.

Gift Giver: Exactly.

Merchant: What? Man, you *are* crazy. *(Turns to other people walking by)* New shirts! Get your shirts over here! Great prices!

Gift Giver: Are you sure you don't want it?

Merchant: Are you still here?

Gift Giver: But it is *worth* your life!

Merchant: Nothing can be worth my life! I like my life just fine! So *no*, I don't want your gift. Give it to someone else!

Gift Giver: *(Starts to walk away)*

Merchant: Hey, buddy . . . just for my curiosity, what is the gift?

Gift Giver: Freedom! *(Continues walking toward offstage, but does not exit.)*

Merchant: *(Shakes his head and looks at the next person)* He should be locked up. Want to buy a shirt? I'll sell it to you for a low price.

(Everyone freezes.)

Gift Giver: *(Walks to center stage)* God's Son, Jesus, said: "If you hold to my teaching, you are really my disciples. Then you will know the truth, and the truth will set you free." They answered him, "We are Abraham's descendants and have never been slaves of any-one. How can you say that we shall be set free?" Jesus replied, "I tell you the truth, everyone who sins is a slave to sin. Now a slave has no permanent place in the family, but a son belongs to it forever. So if the Son sets you free, you will be free indeed" (John 8:31-36).

End

Living Water (a narrated mime)

Synopsis: People are drinking water that leads to death. Jesus offers living water. This ancient Kanji symbol is created by putting two other symbols together. Those two symbols are "Lamb" on top of the symbol for "Person," or put another way, "Lamb over us." This concept translates into the ancient Kanji symbol for "righteousness." It is also another name for Jesus, the righteous Lamb over us.

Target Audience: Adults and teens. Cultures that are familiar with ancient Chinese symbols.

Topic: Salvation

Cast:
Narrator: Speaks loudly and clearly with good intonation
Evil Spirit: Dressed all in black, including gloves
Jesus: Holds a basin
Soldiers: Swords or helmets to get the idea across
Poor Man: Dressed in rags
Young Woman: Normal dress for the culture
Young Man: Dressed as a gang member, or counter-culture

Props: Two basins or bowls. Optional: sand, T-shirts **Optional:** Copy symbol shown. Use iron-on paper to transfer and print symbols onto the front of white T-shirts for Poor Man, Young Man, and Young Woman.

Time: 7 minutes

Difficulty Level: Moderate

Customize:

1. Add more people to drink of the impure water, or add them as background people. Have some people accept Jesus and some deny him.
2. Have white T-shirts given to people, but without any symbol on the front.

Living Water (a narrated mime)

Opening Scene: (*Evil Spirit* is holding a basin of sand and beckoning people to come and drink. Stage left.)

Narrator: All people of the world are thirsty. Evil spirits beckon all people of the world to quench their thirst with impure water. The people try to resist the evil spirits, but because of their thirst are compelled to give in to them. The water fills their soul with impure thoughts and deeds. It does not give life, but death.

Poor Man, Young Man, and Young Woman: (*Enter stage left. Stick hands into container of sand, mime taking a drink and washing water over face. They have clear reactions to the nastiness of the sand, but they continue to eat and wash, even though they are repulsed. Repeat while **Narrator** speaks.*)

Narrator: The God who created heaven and earth and sea and everything in them looked down from heaven and saw many people choosing impure things. So he sent his Son to offer a pure drink: living water.

Jesus: (*Enters stage right holding a bowl. Sits down and mimes speaking. Motions people to drink of his water.*)

Narrator: His Son, Jesus, tells them he will cleanse their souls and restore them. He says that when they drink of the living water, their souls will never die, and they will live with God forever.

(*Others sit around **Jesus**, listening*)

Narrator: But some people had grown used to their old ways and led him away to be killed in the city of Jerusalem. God, his Father, allowed them to kill his Son because God planned from the beginning for Jesus to take the people's death upon himself. This is why he is called the Lamb of God. "He was led as a sheep to the slaughter. As a lamb before his shearer is silent, so he doesn't open his mouth."

Soldiers: (*Enter and drag **Jesus** away off stage right, still holding the bowl.*)

Narrator: But God is merciful and just. He raised Jesus back to life. Many people witnessed this, and they were overjoyed! Many people accepted Jesus' living water and were accepted into God's kingdom as righteous.

Jesus:	*(Enters stage right, and people run to him.)*
Poor Man, Young Man, and Young Woman:	*(All three run to **Jesus** and hold out hands to him, getting on their knees to ask **Jesus** for the living water. Optional: He gives it to them and gives them a T-shirt they put on. They stand up joyfully.)*
Narrator:	The cloth of righteousness is a symbol of purity, which can only be provided through Jesus, the Living Water. This was foretold before time began. This ancient symbol bears witness to this as the "Lamb" over us. *(Points toward shirts.)*
Poor Man, Young Man, and Young Woman:	*(Walk to the front of stage and stand looking at everyone, smiling. Optional: As the **Narrator** reads, point to top of symbol on T-shirt, which stands for "lamb," and then point to bottom of symbol which stands for "us." Hold arms outstretched.)*
Narrator:	All who drink of this living water are so joyful; they want to offer the living water to all people of the world. Will you take his offering?

End

King's Palace (a narrated mime)

Synopsis: An allegory for salvation and the kingdom of God. The kingdom of Zahir is being attacked, and the king sends his son, Prince Zahi, to make peace.

Target Audience: Children of any culture. The names "Salah Rafi" and "Zahi" are Arabic for "exalted righteousness" and "radiance/purity."

Topics: Salvation, Grace

Cast:
King Salah Rafi: Represents God. Should be your tallest actor
Prince Zahi: Represents Jesus
Town Crier: Should have engaging personality
Knight of Nassir: Ability to show sorrow, crying
Princesses, Knights, Nobles, Children: Extras who come into the king's court. Ideally use lots of extras

Props: Throne, red robe for Jesus, cardboard swords

Time: 10 minutes

Difficulty Level: Moderate

Customize:

1. Change names to those that are commonly used in the culture.
2. Make this a script by having characters say the narrator's lines.
3. Make costumes for all characters, add props to king's court.
4. Like most of these skits, you should plan on having a discussion time with your audience to talk about the significance of the allegory.

King's Palace (a narrated mime)

Opening Scene: *(Throne is positioned stage right and facing stage left. Action should happen as the **Narrator** speaks.)*

Narrator: In a land far away there is a kingdom called Zahir, which means radiant. In the kingdom of Zahir, King Salah Rafi lives with his son, Prince Zahi, in the Palace of Grace. This king is different from any other king you may have heard of because he is the king over every other king on earth.

*(**King Salah Rafi** enters and sits on his throne. **Prince Zahi** stands at his right. Both look stage left.)*

Narrator: The King and his son are very just and rule their kingdom with wisdom and truth, for there is no falsehood in the kingdom of Zahir. The Prince is attended by twelve high nobles and many knights who have bravely fought in battle. Princesses come and go within the court of the king, singing songs, bringing food for the king, and sitting at his feet to listen to him speak for he is very wise. Many children also live in the king's castle because the king especially loves and cherishes all children.

*(**Nobles** walk in from stage left in a line and attend to the **Prince**. **Knights** walk in and kneel before the **King**. **Princesses** walk in carrying food and singing, and some sit at the foot of the throne. **Children** enter and also sit at the **King's** throne.)*

Narrator: One day, the Town Crier came running into the palace and requested to speak to the king. The king gave him permission to speak. He said "News has come from the wasteland. The people from the Barrens are planning to attack the kingdom!"

*(**Town Crier** comes running up from stage left and bows down before the **King**. Then he lifts his head and mimes speaking.)*

Narrator: King Salah Rafi said "This is terrible news. Don't they know they can't possibly win? Go and gather all the people and bring them into the palace." Then he called the high nobles together and told them to assemble all the men of the kingdom. He presented his son, Prince Zahi, with a red sash and asked him to lead the men and protect the kingdom.

*(**King** stands and places the sash on the **Prince**.)*

Narrator: The king paced back and forth in his palace as he awaited news of the advancing army. The king loves all people on the earth—because he is the king of kings of all the earth—and it saddened him to see people who wanted to tear down his kingdom.

(**King** paces back and forth next to his throne, stopping to think for a few seconds and continuing to pace.)

Narrator: The Town Crier approached the king's court with more news of the approaching army. "My Lord, I bring you sad news. Your son . . . Prince Zahi . . . he has been . . . captured."

(**Town Crier** comes walking in quickly and bows, then mimes talking.)

Narrator: The King said, "Take heart. All is not lost."

(The **King** looks down at the **Town Crier** and puts his hand on his shoulder. Then **Town Crier** walks away.)

Narrator: A few moments later, the Knight of Nassir ["Nassir" means "protector"] came into the king's court. He said "If it pleases the king, I have brought you Prince Zahi's robe. My Lord, they beat and whipped your son. They gave him a crown of thorns and used a cruel form of punishment . . . My Lord . . . they hammered two long nails through his hands and . . . hung him on a crossbeam made of wood.

Knight of Nassir: (Enters stage left. He walks straight and tall but stops a few steps from the throne. Then he advances a few more steps. Reports to the **King**, starting to cry partway through. Then slumps down on the floor in front of the throne.)

Narrator: Prince Zahi's name means pure, and the king knew he did not deserve this cruel punishment. For three days and nights he stayed seated on his throne waiting. He pondered his kingdom, and his heart welled up with love. Love for all the people of the entire world, including those who killed his son.

(The **King** sits in his chair, while slowly, women and children walk in to wait with the **King**.)

Narrator: On the morning of the third day, everyone in the kingdom crowded into King Salah Rafi's court. They were excited and laughing as they approached the king. All bowed down before the throne. The Town Crier stood and said, "King Salah Rafi, our most mighty and righteous judge, who is gracious and compassionate, slow to anger and abounding in love, we have good news!"

(All the people of the court enter and are talking. Some mime playing recorders and shaking tambourines. Then they all bow low on the ground.)

Narrator: King Salah Rafi said "Approach, Town Crier, and give me this good news."

*(**King Salah Rafi** gestures with his hand for the **Town Crier** to approach.)*

Narrator: The Town Crier said, "We have witnessed a miracle! Your son, Prince Zahi, is alive! We have seen him and spoken with him. He has gone into the camps of the enemy and walked throughout the kingdom. He is coming to the court wearing a long white robe and a golden sash. His hair is white, and his face shines like the sun!"

*(**Town Crier** stands and mimes speaking excitedly to the **King**.)*

Narrator: All the people in the court and beyond gave a loud yell: "Hurray! He lives! Prince Zahi lives!" "But there is more, my king," the Crier said. "When the people of the Barrens saw Prince Zahi walk through their camps, they threw down their sabers and bowed low before him! They have given themselves over to you and are ready for the judgment they deserve for the cruelty they gave your son."

*(Everyone gets up and jumps around hugging each other, raising their hands. The **Town Crier** turns and mimes speaking again to the **King**.)*

Narrator: The court become very quiet as they awaited word from the king. King Salah Rafi rose and said, "Since the days of old when men turned away from me to seek their own pleasure, I have longed to be reunited with them. But they have been a rebellious people not wanting to seek my wisdom and rule of their lives, though I loved them with an everlasting love. Now they have done the ultimate evil and have killed my son. But what they meant for evil, I turned into good, for my name means good. I have brought my son back to life. He has taken the punishment for all. Whoever repents and believes in my son can come and live with me in the kingdom of Zahir, for eternity. Go and bring the people of the Barrens into the palace and prepare a great feast! We will celebrate their return!"

*(**King** stands and speaks to the court.)*

Narrator: And all the people of the Kingdom of Zahir celebrated and honored King Salah Rafi. Each day King Salah Rafi looks out his window with his son, Prince Zahi, watching for his beloved people to return home.

*(Everyone excitedly runs around and then exits, except the **King** and **Prince**, who stand serenely looking offstage left.)*

End

Walls (a narrated mime)

Synopsis: Jesus has the ability to restore broken relationships.

Target Audience: Adults, teens, and children. Simple message of reconciliation that speaks to all cultures and religions.

Topics: Forgiveness, Restoration

Cast:

Three children: Can be played by youth
Husband and Wife: Easy parts to play for anyone
Father and Son: Easy parts to play for anyone
Jesus: An easy part

Props: None

Time: 3 minutes

Difficulty Level: Easy

Customize: We have used three very common relationships in this skit. If there are situations that are specific to your church or to the region you are witnessing in, replace these generic relationships with more specific ones that are meaningful to your audience.

Walls (a narrated mime)

Opening Scene: *(Two of the **Children**, the **Father** and **Son**, **Husband** and **Wife** are all standing onstage. The two **Children** are downstage center, and behind them are the **Husband** and **Wife**, and then behind them (upstage center) are the **Father** and **Son**.)*

Narrator: Two children play together. They are close friends and share everything. One day a new girl moves into their neighborhood. The girls get jealous, and they start to argue. Their friendship is broken.

*(Two **Children** are sitting and playing patty-cake downstage center. Another **Child** enters, and one **Child** stops playing and starts to play with the new **Child**. The new **Child** switches between them. They argue and turn their backs to each other and take four steps away.)*

Narrator: A husband and wife are in love. They do everything together and look forward to having a family together. But as time goes by, little things start to bother them, and they start to argue. Soon, they are arguing every day and thinking about divorce.

*(**Husband** and **Wife** are standing center stage looking at each other talking and laughing. The **Wife** points at the ground and then at him and puts her hands on her hips. The **Husband** throws his hands in the air and points at her. They argue, both cross their arms and turn their backs on each other. They walk three steps away.)*

Narrator: A father and son are very close. They enjoy talking about sports and playing basketball together. As the son grows older, he disagrees with his father on many things, and they start to argue. Every time they talk, they argue. They don't even like the same sports anymore.

*(**Father** and **Son** are standing upstage center talking and laughing. **Father** puts his hand on boy's shoulder as they talk. They motion dribbling and playing basketball. The **Son** then puts his hands on his hips, and the **Father** wags his finger at his **Son**. They start to argue and finally turn their backs on each other and take two steps away.)*

Narrator: Jesus Christ comes to forgive us all. When we believe in and receive his forgiveness, he gives us the ability to forgive others. Jesus came to break down the walls people build between each other, to restore families, to restore love, to rebuild relationships. He came to bridge the gap between you and God. The Bible says, "Today, if you hear his voice, do not harden your hearts . . ."

(**Jesus** enters while **Narrator** is talking and brings the relationships back together by taking their hands and putting them into each other's. The **Father** and **Son** turn and walk toward each other and then hug patting each other on the back. The **Husband** and **Wife** turn and walk up to each other; they hold hands and smile. The **Children** turn and walk toward each other. They start to play jump-rope.)

End

The Door to Life Abundant (a mime)

Synopsis: Acted-out adaptation of the Four Spiritual Laws (1. God loves us. 2. We are sinful and separated from God. 3. Jesus is the only path to God. 4. We must recognize Jesus as Lord and Savior to get back into right relationship with God.)

Target Audience: Adults, youth, and children. Speaks to all cultures and religious practices with the very basic salvation message

Topics: Salvation, Bridge to God

Cast:

Jesus: Dressed in modern-day clothing, colors of royalty or purity

Woman: In her twenties. Goes back and forth looking for doorway or door handle.

Man: Middle-aged businessman, just bangs on wall over and over in same place. Uses feet and briefcase also

Teen Girl: Persistent. Tries many ways to get over wall, including looking under it

Teen Boy: Athlete. Tries to jump over, uses pole vault, pushes desk over to wall, tries ladder, and stretches in between attempts

Old Woman: Slowly walks up to door and bangs on it with her cane

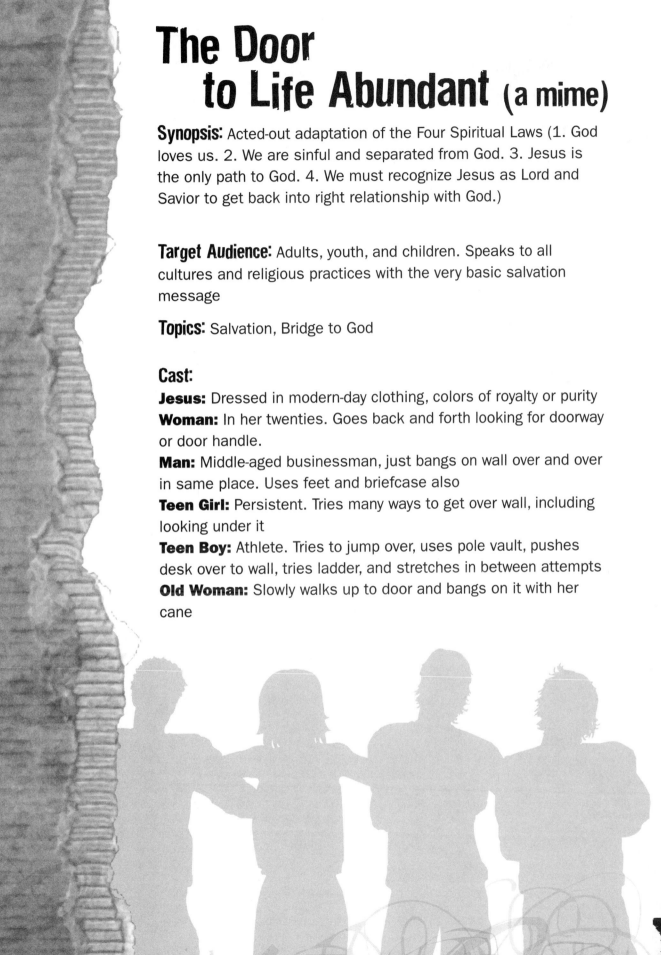

Props: Briefcase, cane

Time: 5 minutes

Difficulty Level: Easy

Customize: You can break up the skit at its different, logical points to discuss each of the four spiritual laws. Feel free to get in-depth or use personal testimony to elaborate on each law.

The Door to Life Abundant (a mime)

Opening Scene: *(The cast is scattered across the stage left and center areas. They should act as if there's an invisible wall separating them from the right area of the stage.)*

Narrator: The Lord God, who created everything, loves you and has an amazing plan for your life. For God so loved the world that he gave his only begotten Son, that whoever believes in him will not perish but have everlasting life. His Son, Jesus, said, "I came that they would have life and have it to the full."

(People kneel down, hold out arms to sky looking up, and then hold arms to chest to show they are looking for love.)

Narrator: Why don't people experience the great life God has planned for them? Because all people of the world have free choice to act how they want, and this separates them from God.

(The same people turn and are arguing and fighting with each other, yelling, kicking, pushing, stealing, and running, etc.)

Narrator: All people fall short of God's perfection. Not one person is kind enough or good enough to be with God. They are separated from God for all eternity.

(All people walk over to stage right and come up against a wall. Act out trying to get to the other side as described per their character. Then all the people get down on their knees where they are, put their head in their hands or arms and cry.)

Narrator: God loves people so much that he sent his Son, Jesus, to tell people how to receive and know God's love. Jesus said, "I am the way, the truth, and the life, no one comes to the Father, but through me." And then, when people didn't understand, Jesus paid the penalty for their bad choices.

*(**Jesus** enters stage left. He walks through the people. The people get up as he passes them. When he gets to the "wall," he turns and faces them. He puts his arms up as though on a cross and then walks through the wall. Everyone gasps, putting their hands to their mouth or chest. Then they walk quickly to the wall. Jesus turns and faces them again, now on the other side of the wall.)*

Narrator: Jesus is the door to reach God. He says, "Behold I stand at the door and knock; if anyone hears my voice and opens the door, I will come in to him."

*(**Teen Girl** walks up in front of **Jesus** with the wall in between them and knocks. **Jesus** opens the door and welcomes her in, gesturing with arm and smiling. The **Teen Girl** walks through, hugs **Jesus**, and bows down low. **Businessman** does the same, slowly and unsure. The **Teen Boy** runs up excitedly and does the same. When they are all bowed down, they then all get up and are excited and happy.)*

Narrator: People who let Jesus be their advocate can now have a relationship with God. He no longer holds their failings against them. And now they are open to receive God's Spirit which helps them live more abundant lives than they had before. They can now live with God forever.

*(The **Young** and **Old Woman** on the other side are sad or angry. The people on **Jesus**' side of the wall open the door and walk over to them and gesture for them to enter. The **Old Woman** does and receives the joy of salvation. The **Young Woman** doesn't and continues searching for a way to the other side of the wall.)*

Narrator: You can receive this free gift of abundant life by accepting your own inadequacies, and trusting in God, through Jesus, to help you to a more fulfilling life. If any of you in the audience would like to take God up on his offer, please come forward for prayer.

End

Angels: Part 1—Married

Synopsis: Two angels talk about the day's events and end up reminiscing about Jesus' birth

Target Audience: Adult and teens. Of particular interest to Muslims and Americans who focus on angels. Also for those Europeans and Americans who are nominal Christians.

Topics: Angels, God's Sovereignty

Cast:

Angelo: Outgoing male angel. Friendly, able to speak loudly onstage, great intonation and feeling. Can be dressed in white, or use a unique application of face paint to convey his nature

Angelica: Female angel. Loud, joyful, self-confident, contagious personality. Can be dressed in white, or use a unique application of face paint to convey her nature.

Rebecca: Eighteen-year-old girl, unsure of herself. Good acting ability

John: Twenty-year-old guy, confident but kind. Good acting ability

Sue: Rebecca's older sister. Good acting ability

Bill: Co-worker of John. Good acting ability

Mary: Mother of Jesus, needs to look pregnant, dressed in robe. Good acting ability, not much of a speaking part

Joseph: Outgoing, good actor, dressed in robe. Able to act anxious, have good intonation in his voice, good body language using no props. Kind to Mary

Innkeeper: Dressed in robe, loud, forceful character, impatient

Props: Two chairs or stools

Time: 7 minutes

Difficulty Level: Difficult. Numerous lines to memorize

Customize: Angelo can be the facilitator for an audience discussion during the intermission.

Angels: Part 1—Married

Opening Scene: (*Angelica is sitting upstage center, head in her hands, looking like she's down.*)

Angelo: (*Enters stage right. Walks over to **Angelica**) Hey! (They engage in a complicated greeting ritual. [Feel free to make something up. Long and silly is okay.]*) Why were you looking so down before?

Angelica: Oh, I don't know. Angel school didn't prepare me for being so underappreciated. I have spent a lot of time with Rebecca, protecting her from accidents and from falling, but she isn't very thankful.

Angelo: Yeah? Well, I actually became visible to John the other day. He was traveling to visit a friend and was going to take this long winding road that would have led to disaster at that time of night, so I appeared to him as a truck driver and warned him about that road. Thankfully, he took my advice.

Angelica: That's a good thing! I think they expect us to appear in front of them every day, answering all their prayers the way they want!

Angelo: Oh, it's not all bad! These humans are amazing creatures made in God's image!

Angelica: I love how much they laugh! Just the other day, Rebecca and her sister were joking up a storm. (***Angels** step back and observe the scene as it's happening.*)

Sue: (*Walks in from stage left with her sister **Rebecca**. They are both laughing hard.*) I can't believe you said that!

Rebecca: Well, I have to say it like it is . . . (*Keeps laughing then calms down*) Anyway, what should I do? Should I get a job?

Sue: What are your choices?

Rebecca: Not many I guess. Taking care of a baby is so hard! Now that I've graduated high school, I guess I need a full time job. I don't understand why God can't let me win the lottery.

Sue: It's because the other players already sold their souls to Satan so they could win.

Rebecca: I guess.

Sue: I think your biggest problem is that you haven't prayed about it yet.

Rebecca: OK . . . that would be nice. You're a great sis. (**Sue** *takes her sister's hand and walks offstage left.*)

Angelica: She keeps going, no matter how hard it gets.

Angelo: Yes, and John too . . . he has such integrity! Even when that tempting situation came along at work, he didn't cross that line. Pretty good for a twenty-year-old. (**Angels** *step back and observe the scene as it's happening.*)

John: (*Walks in stage left with his co-worker,* **Bill***.*)

Bill: Thanks John, I appreciate all your help on this project.

John: Anytime.

Bill: Hey, one more thing, I've got this problem with money.

John: Yeah?

Bill: Yeah . . . I was wondering if you could take some out of the till for me. You know, a loan.

John: I'm not sure . . .

Bill: (*Laughs*) It's OK; no one will find out. (*Laughs again*)

John: Hey, funny one, Bill. You know I'm just a clerk . . . you had me for a minute (*Looks at watch*) Gotta run. (*Walks off stage left*)

Bill: John, wait, I really need . . . (*Walks off following him*)

Angelo: He works hard every week; then he helps out with the youth group on weekends. The same youth group he grew up in.

Angelica: He and Rebecca would be a great match.

Angelo: Well, I came over here to tell you something! It's a secret.

Angelica: A secret! What are you waiting for . . . tell me!

Angelo: God took me aside the other day and said he had a plan for John and Rebecca to get married!

Angelica: No way, that's great news! When's the big event?

Angelo: He didn't tell me. But he said I need to help them meet. The enemy is planning to stop it.

Angelica: It reminds me of Mary and Joseph. Remember when they had to travel so far with Mary being pregnant?

Angelo: Yeah, and riding a donkey!

Angelica: And they had nowhere to stay? Satan tried to mess up the Savior's birth by booking up all of Bethlehem.

Angelo: The birth of Jesus was going to happen no matter what! God's plans for humanity always prevail!

Angelica: Even though we knew the innkeeper would turn them away, it was still hard to believe when it actually happened! Can you imagine? (*Angels* step back and observe the scene as it's happening.)

(*Mary* and *Joseph* enter stage left. *Joseph* takes her by the hand and leads her upstage center.)

Joseph: (*Knocks on door*) Hey, anyone in there? My wife is pregnant and about to give birth! Anyone around? (*Peeks in through window. Walks a little further*) Hell-ooo, anyone home? Is there any place we can stay for the night?

Mary: (*Takes hold of* **Joseph's** *sleeve.*) Let's try the inn over there.

Joseph: (*Turns around and leads her back toward stage left*) Mary, don't worry, we'll find someplace to sleep. Even if it's in someone's cart.

Mary: Oh, no! What if it rains?

Joseph: That's true . . . maybe this innkeeper will take us. (*Knocks on door.* **Innkeeper** *enters stage left.*)

Innkeeper: Can I help you?

Joseph: Yes, thank you! My wife, Mary, is about to give birth. We've been looking everywhere for a place to stay. Do you have any rooms?

Innkeeper: No! So many people have come by looking for rooms! Do you know how many I have turned away today?

Joseph: Please, I have money to pay. We won't give you any trouble. A roof, somewhere? For my wife?

Innkeeper: W-e-l-l, I do have one place. Follow me. (*Grabs his lantern, and they follow him offstage left.*)

Angelo: I know . . . he sent them out back to the cave where he kept the animals. Boy, did it smell in there! Whew!

Angelica: Mary didn't even seem to notice.

Angelo: That's because her nose was running.

Angelica: Now that was some night! When I think of how much God loves the humans he created . . . He actually sent his Son to earth to live with them . . . (*Angelica's watch alarm goes off.*) Oh! Rebecca's about to do something accident-prone. Gotta run. (*Angelica runs offstage right.*)

Angelo: Later then.

Intermission.

Angels: Part 2—Meeting

Synopsis: Two angels talk about the day's events and reminisce about Jesus' birth.

Target Audience: Adults and teens. Of particular interest to Muslims and Americans who focus on angels. Also for Europeans who are often nominal Christians.

Topics: Angels, Salvation, Jesus

Cast:
Angelo: Male angel who's outgoing, friendly, able to speak loud onstage, great intonation and feeling
Angelica: Female angel who's a little less outgoing, obviously enjoys friendship with Angelo
John: Twenty-year-old guy, confident but kind. Good acting ability
Rebecca: Eighteen-year-old girl, unsure of herself. Good acting ability
Mary 1: Bible-time Mary dressed in a robe, sandals, carrying a basket, good acting ability, good expressions
Mary 2: Bible-time Mary dressed in a robe, sandals, carrying a basket, good acting ability, good expressions

Time: 7 minutes

Props: Two chairs or stools, two baskets

Difficulty Level: Difficult. Numerous lines to memorize

Angels: Part 2—Meeting

Opening Scene: (*Angelica standing upstage center talking on cell phone*)

Angelo: (*Walks in stage left*) I can't believe you're using that thing!

Angelica: (*Laughs*) Good to see you! (*They engage in a complicated greeting ritual. [Feel free to make something up. Long and silly is okay.]*) I just spent some time with Rebecca in the hospital.

Angelo: Oh? Did she have another mishap?

Angelica: Yes! Can you believe it? That girl is prone to accidents!

Angelo: Well, I just got through watching over John as he was buying the ring.

Angelica: What's it look like? (*Joking*) A one-carat diamond?

Angelo: (*Sincerely*) Only the best!

Angelica: Uh-huh. I'm looking forward to the wedding! Seems like only yesterday we were talking about God's plan for them to meet.

Angelo: I know! Time flies . . . and so do we.

Angelica: As I was saying . . . Rebecca came into the church that night . . . (***Angels** step back and observe the scene as it's happening.*)

(***Rebecca** walks in stage left and stands looking around. **John** enters stage right, walks toward her while looking and waving to someone behind him.*)

John: OK, thanks for the directions! (*He walks right into **Rebecca**, who falls over.*) Oh, I'm so sorry! (*Gives her a hand up*) I wasn't watching where I was going.

Rebecca: It's OK. Maybe it was my fault. I was just standing here not knowing where to go.

John: Are you new here?

Rebecca: Yes, it's my first night.

John: You're early. It doesn't start for another hour.

Rebecca: Really? But the brochure said . . .

John: 7:00? I just heard they had a pipe break in the building, so it's starting late. Want to grab a coffee while we wait?

Rebecca: Um, I'm not sure.

John: Don't worry, I'm not an ax murderer. Pretty normal guy, really. *(Takes her arm and leads her offstage left.)*

Angelo: It's amazing the way God wove events in their lives to fulfill his plans.

Angelica: While we're reminiscing, remember when those shepherds who were on the hill saw the star and followed it to where Jesus was born? I bet they were shocked! God knew they would be so struck with awe and wonder. I bet they never thought it would lead to a cow stall!

Angelo: *(Laughs)* The human saying is true, big things sometimes do come in small packages. Well, I would never think of having Jesus born like that, in those circumstances. But then, I'm not God.

Angelica: How else would God get across the idea that Jesus came to serve and save the lost? It was perfect! A perfect place to be born...

Angelo: And after hundreds of years of preparation, a perfect time! The timing is what is so hard to grasp. God, in all his omniscience, knew that he would be rejected by so many . . .

Angelica: *(Steps forward and speaks as if orating)* Knew that Barabbas would be traded for Jesus...

Angelo: *(Steps forward and speaks as if orating)* Knew that Jesus would be sentenced to death!

Angelica: How he must have grieved . . . to see his Son beaten, nails hammered into his hands, hanging in agony on a cross, unjustly killed.

Angelo: And for what?

Angelica: Healing the sick, giving sight to the blind, feeding the multitudes!

Angelo: Remember the look on that little boy's face when he realized his basket of five loaves and two fishes fed five thousand people? I laughed and laughed when I saw that! *(Starts laughing)*

Angelica: What a life he lived!

Angelo: How about when the two Marys saw that Jesus was not in the tomb? (**Angels** step back and observe the scene as it's happening.)

Marys: *(Walk onstage left. Stop and stare. Drop baskets and run over to downstage center.)*

Mary 1: Mary look! It's empty!

Mary 2: *(Runs over)* Where is Jesus?? Who took him??

Angelo: *(Gets up and walks over to them. The* **Marys** *grab each other's arms in fear as the angel talks, and take a step back)* Do not be afraid, for I know that you are looking for Jesus, who was crucified. He is not here; he has risen, just as he said. Come and see the place where he lay. Then go quickly and tell his disciples: "He has risen from the dead and is going ahead of you into Galilee. There you will see him." Now I have told you.

Angelica: *(Starts reciting in unison with* **Angelo**.*)* He has risen from the dead and is going ahead of you into Galilee. There you will see him. Now I have told you.

Marys: Hurry, Jesus is alive! We must tell the others. *(They pick up their baskets and run away offstage left.)*

Angelica: *(Walks back over to* **Angelo**.*)* The miracle of how Jesus rose from the grave, to save men from their sin…

Angelo: It was all part of God's plan from the beginning.

Angelica: Well, we better go. I have to see how Rebecca is doing with all the wedding plans!! Umm, I mean, guard her house tonight.

Angelo: Uh, huh. See you at the wedding.

(Walk offstage right together)

End

Chains

Synopsis: Humorous adaptation of Acts 16 when Paul and Silas are in prison

Target Audience: Adults and teens

Topics: Salvation, Witnessing

Cast:

Paul: Well spoken, humble, great acting ability

Silas: Energetic, open companion of Paul, a little rash, great acting ability

Guard: Good actor

Prisoner 1: Very old man with long beard, crazy from being in prison so long. Speaks with rough voice

Prisoner 2: Ship captain who was thrown in prison only a few days earlier. Big man who has seen one too many hard times. Rough looking and talking

Props: Chains for prisoners, spear, sword

Time: 7 minutes

Difficulty Level: Difficult

Customize: As the actors mention someone not in the scene, have that person enter stage left, act out their part, and exit stage left. For example, have the possessed girl walk on stage, say her lines, and then back offstage. At the beginning, you could also include the guard's monologue regarding his name. Have Mamillia Bovinne enter, then his family, then someone walks on and gives Mamillia a treasure chest.

Chains

Opening Scene: *(Paul and Silas get pushed into a prison by a Guard stage right. There are other prisoners sitting around inside, chained up.)*

Guard: Get in there you two. *(Pushes Paul and Silas in one at a time.)*

Silas: Hey, *(Turning and facing Guard)* who do you think you are?

Guard: *(Stands straight and hits fist to chest)* I'm Gluteus Maximus, high guard of the noble court of his honorable and venerable magistrate, Sir Mamillia Bovinne, of the Family of Suse, appointed heir to the family treasures at Lystra.

Silas: Can I just call you Glute?

Guard: *(Relaxes, smiles)* That's what my brother calls me.

Silas: Well, Glute, we have a situation here. *(Puts hands on hips)*

Paul: *(Walks over)* Silas, we better let the man do his job. *(Gestures to the guard)* Now come along, Gluteus. Where are those stocks you promised us?

Guard: *(Stiffens up again)* Right. Down there, you two. *(Pushes them with his spear)*

(Paul and Silas get down on the ground and wait for Guard to put chains on their feet. Guard exits.)

Silas: I could have talked him into letting us go, you know. He was warming up to me.

Prisoner 1: Hee, hee, heeeee! *(High-pitched laughter)*

Paul: Maybe. I didn't think casting that demon out of the servant girl would end with us in prison.

Silas: You were getting tired of her repeating herself. Why did she keep following us?

Paul: To torment us, I guess. How many times could we hear her say, *(Mocking voice)* "These are servants of the Highest God. They are telling you how to be saved from the punishment of sin"?

Prisoner 1: *(Mocking)* Servants of the most high, servants of the most high, servants of the most high…

(**Paul** and **Silas** look over to **Prisoner 1**.)

Silas: *(Still looking at man)* Gets on your nerves after awhile.

Paul: It made our witnessing harder!

Silas: *(Looks back at **Paul**)* You can say that again.

Paul: Yeah, that's an awful bruise on your forehead.

Prisoner 2: You think that's bad. Ha! You should see the one they gave me! Wacked me right across the stomach I tell you, sliced it open so my guts were pouring out. I'd be lucky to be alive if I weren't in this hole!

Paul: What did you do to get sliced up like that?

Prisoner 2: Oh never mind that. I'm sure I've seen you two before . . .

Prisoner 1: At the bottom of the deep blue sea.

Paul: *(To **Prisoner 2**)* Oh?

Silas: *(To **Paul**)* Getting hit with sticks does tend to cause bruising.

Paul: Got a few on my backside I'd like to be rid of.

Prisoner 1: Hee, hee, heeeee! *(High pitched laughter)* Backside boys.

Silas: I'm afraid my tooth got knocked out, too.

Prisoner 1: *(Opens his mouth wide and sticks his fingers in feeling for teeth.)*

Paul: *(Laughs a little)* Just one?

Prisoner 1: Ha! Why a few years back I had three teeth knocked out during a skirmish in Nineveh. Nasty town.

Silas: *(To **Paul**)* So, how many times have you been beaten now?

Prisoner 2: About twenty-two, I'd say.

Prisoner 1: *(Holds up hands and starts to count one finger at a time. Shakes his head and starts over.)*

Silas: No, not you!

Paul: Too many times to count. But it isn't anything compared to what I did, you know. The people I used to torment and kill . . .

Prisoner 1: Kill and torment, kill and torment, kill and torment. *(In a lighthearted sing-song voice)*

Silas: What was it like, seeing Jesus?

Prisoner 2: That's where I've seen you two! You were on the ship sailing from Troas.

Paul: That's right. Were you the captain, then?

Prisoner 2: You remember. Sorry about all that back there.

Silas: *(Tries to get up)* You!

Paul: *(Pulls him down)* It's all right. He's locked up now.

Prisoner 2: Yeah, just like you two . . . ha, ha, ha.

Silas: I can't believe this! Locked in here with him! *(Looks his way)* You tried to throw us overboard!

Prisoner 1: Ahhhyyeee, sink or swim, sink or swim! *(Tries to get away, using swimming motions with arms)*

Prisoner 2: Well, your God came to the rescue. *(Looks down disappointedly)*

Paul: What were we talking about? Oh yes, my experience seeing Jesus. I can't quite describe it. There was a blinding light! So blinding I actually became blind . . . couldn't see for three whole days.

Silas: Did you ever wonder why God chose you?

Paul: Me? Oh . . . of course. But he chooses whom he chooses. I think maybe because of my great sin.

Prisoner 2: He should have chosen me then! Ha ha, the sins I've committed (Slaps hand on knee) There was this woman . . .

Silas: None of that!

Prisoner 1: Hee, hee, heee. None of that girly talk in this respectable establishment.

Paul: A man named Ananias prayed for me in Damascus, and my sight returned! He said "What are you waiting for? Get up and be baptized. Have your sins washed away by calling on the name of the Lord!"

Silas: And here you are!

Prisoner 1: *(Mocking voice)* These are servants of the Highest God.

Prisoner 2: Yeah, here you are, stuck in this hell hole with me! Ha, ha, ha.

Prisoner 1: *(Starts singing)* Stuck in the middle with you, stuck in the middle with you . . .

Paul: Yes . . . and here we are! Thank you for being faithful, Silas. *(Slaps hands on legs)* It must be around midnight. Now, let's sing praises to God and pray this will not set us back for too long.

Silas: *(Starts singing, and **Paul** joins him.)* Amazing grace, how sweet the sound . . .

*(Things start to shake in the room. **Paul** and **Silas** and others are shaken around.)*

Silas: Look! *(Pointing offstage right)* The prison door—it's open!

Paul: Our chains are broken, too.

(They stand up and brush off the dust.)

Guard: *(Rushes in. Drops spear in fear. Puts hands to face)* No! I'm a disgrace! *(Pulls out sword)*

Prisoner 1: Free, free, free! (In a sing-song voice, stooped over, crazily running around prison)

Paul: No, don't kill yourself! None of us will run away. *(Glances at **Prisoner 2**)*

Prisoner 1: *(Stops and stares, stooped over)*

Prisoner 2: *(Stands in disbelief, but doesn't leave.)*

Guard: *(Comes into prison cell and kneels down on one knee in front of **Paul**.)* What must I do to be saved?

Paul: *(Puts a hand on the man's shoulder)* Put your trust in the Lord Jesus Christ, and you and your family will be saved from the punishment of sin.

End

Baggage (a mime)

Synopsis: Man goes through life sinning against people. Those people follow him through life. He finds Jesus can break the bondage of his sin.

Target Audience: Adults and teens. All cultures can relate to carrying around their past.

Topics: Sin, Salvation, Bondage

Cast:
Man: Typical middle-class man
Two Teens: Scared, weak
Wife: Talkative, forceful, and angry
Boss: Very direct and sure of himself
Clerk: Young adult, impatient
Jesus: Can dress normally, in colors of royalty or purity

Props: Purse, coat, glasses, newspaper

Time: 5 minutes

Difficulty Level: Easy

Customize:
1. For English-speaking people, instead of a mime, add script to each scene.
2. Create more characters and situations so the line is very long.
3. Add narration in between scenes.
4. Change the scenes to represent problems that are the most prevalent sins in that culture.

Baggage (a mime)

Opening Scene: (*Man* enters stage left. After every confrontation he walks around the stage in a large circle to get across the idea he is traveling through time and distance.)

Two Teens: (*Enter stage right*)

Man and Teens: (*Man* walks up to **Teens** and gets into a fight, beating them both. They lie on the ground moaning. He picks up his hat and puts it back on and walks across the stage. Two **Teens** get up and start following **Man** walking in a line behind him.)

Man and Wife: (*Man* starts arguing with **Wife**. She starts crying. He turns his back on her with arms crossed. She picks up her purse, puts on her coat, and walks off stage. He gestures good riddance with his hand and picks up the paper to read. Puts down paper and walks out the door, keeps walking. Two **Teens** are still following and now **Wife** walks onstage and follows behind **Teens**. All in a line behind **Man**.)

Man and Boss: (*Boss* enters stage. **Man** walks up to **Boss**. **Boss** pulls out a book and starts to ask questions, pointing aggressively at the book and at **Man**. **Man** shrugs his shoulders and shakes his head no, but **Boss** persists. **Man** tells **Boss** he quits and walks off angrily. **Boss** shakes his head and turns away. Then he turns back and walks behind **Wife**.)

Man and Clerk: (*Clerk* enters stage. **Man** walks into a store and asks **Clerk** how much for an item. **Clerk** tells him and **Man** pulls his pockets inside out to show he has no money. **Clerk** shakes his head no, and turns around to stock the shelves. **Man** steals the item and walks out the door. **Clerk** walks around and sees the item is missing. He walks out the door and starts following **Boss**.)

Man and Jesus: (*Jesus* enters stage. **Man** walks up to **Jesus**. **Jesus** points to the people behind **Man**. **Man** looks briefly and shakes his head no. **Jesus** again shows him the people behind him. **Jesus** walks with him to each one. **Man** walks over to each one and looks hard. He looks more and more upset until he gets to the two **Teens**. Then he starts to cry.)

(**Jesus** puts his hand on **Man's** shoulders and gestures for **Man** to admit his sin. **Man** looks at the people and nods his head yes. Then he falls at **Jesus'** feet and holds up his hands. **Jesus** nods his head yes. **Man** stands and hugs **Jesus**, smiling joyfully.)

(**Man** walks to each person and asks their forgiveness. Each person says yes, gives him a hug and walks offstage left or right. **Jesus** and **Man** walk offstage together smiling and talking.)

End

On the Run

Synopsis: People are hurrying about, worried about many things, and don't take time to listen to God. This skit should lead into a message or testimony.

Target Audience: Adults and youth. Cultures that are hurrying—urban.

Topics: Seeking God, Peace

Cast:
Megan: Peaceful woman, undisturbed by the activity around her
Michael: Always running late for everything! Harried
Seth: Anxiously looking for his friend who is always late
Jasmine: Impatient and upset
Charlie: Extremely busy and overloaded
Elizabeth: Worried about all her homework and exams

Props: Table, chair, Bible, fork (follow cultural norm i.e., chopsticks), place-setting

Time: 3 minutes

Difficulty Level: Easy

Customize:
1. This is a great skit for kids to ad-lib.
2. Have characters memorize the last line in the language of the country you are visiting.

On the Run

Opening Scene: (*Everyone except* **Megan** *is at the back of the audience. As needed, run to the stage, then run off the stage to the back of the room again. Actors can be out of breath.*)

Megan: (*Sitting at a table center stage. She is eating dinner very slowly. She picks up her Bible every so often and reads a verse. She glances at people as they run by.*)

Seth: (*Holding books. Runs onto stage right and stops in the middle.*) Where is he? He said he'd be here! (*Walks around anxiously looking for him*) Oh well, I better go, I'm late anyway! (*Runs off stage left*)

Michael: (*Holding books. Runs onto stage right and stops in the middle*) What time is it? I'm so late. I can't wait for him. (*Pacing back and forth, runs off stage left*)

Jasmine: (*Runs onto stage right and stops in the middle. Looks at watch; dials cell phone*) Hey, where are you? I'm so busy today; I needed that stuff an hour ago! Why can't you ever be on time? Oh fine! (*Runs off stage left*)

Charlie: (*Holding briefcase or bag—runs onstage right. Looks at watch*) What a day! It was so hectic. Seven p.m. and I still have a huge assignment to finish! Oh no, looks like I might miss the bus, too! W-a-i-t! (*Runs off stage left*)

Elizabeth: (*Runs onto stage left shuffling a bunch of papers*) Now where was that? It was right here! I have to find it or I'll fail my class! I have so much homework to do! (*Runs off stage right*)

Megan: (*Leaves tip, gets up, and slowly grabs her purse and Bible*)

Everyone: (*Goes back onstage both right and left running, in a hurry, walking quickly, being upset, looking at watches, calling on phone. Eventually everyone exits, leaving* **Megan** *alone onstage.*)

Megan: *(Walks slowly through the crowd and walks off stage center to the middle of the audience. Stops where everyone in the audience can see and hear her. Takes two steps forward.)* Search me, God, and know my heart; test me and know my anxious thoughts. See if there is any offensive way in me, and lead me in the way everlasting [Psalm 139:23-24]. Be still; God is in control [Psalm 46:10].

End

Director's Notes

154

Director's Notes

Director's Notes

Director's Notes